Praise for *H*

Many Catholics are aware of ...., but far fewer know them as friends and role models for their marriage. *Holier Matrimony* offers a practical and accessible introduction to the many holy men and women who have lived this vocation with heroic virtue throughout the history of the Church, and experienced joys and crosses familiar to every married couple. I would encourage anyone who desires to enrich their marriage or is preparing for that commitment to take this opportunity to meet these saints and follow their example of faithfulness and love.

— **Father Cassidy Stinson,** priest for the Diocese of Richmond, Virginia.

"There is only one sadness, and that is not to be holy." — Léon Blois.

Thank you to Caitrin Bennett for such an inspiring and hopeful book that enables us to escape sadness and respond as a couple to Jesus' call to become saints. Caitrin not only tells us their stories; she also points out the paths that enabled them to reach the highest heights of holiness. Isn't that why the Church brought them to the altars? To show us the way, to make our journey easier, to enable us to imitate them so that we can fulfill our vocation, to go to Heaven — and to go there as a couple and as a family! What a joy!

— **Jean Luc Moens,** first CHARIS moderator, member of the Emmanuel Community, and a personal friend of the Rugambas.

Even if you've read a plethora of books about the saints, this insightful collection of stories about married saints is sure to inspire holiness and deepen your relationship with your spouse.

— **Michelle Buckman,** editor and author of *Rachel's Contrition.*

Holier Matrimony offers stories about saintly spouses and parents who serve as an inspiration for the lay faithful striving to answer the call to holiness within the Domestic Church. The stories of married saints, the discussion and reflection questions, and the emphasis on the varying promises made via the marriage vows make this book an invaluable guide for engaged and married couples seeking saintly wisdom. Caitrin Bennett's book will help inspire the faithful to persevere in marriage "in good times and in bad."

— **Roland Millare, STD,** vice president of curriculum for the St. John Paul II Foundation, and author of *A Living Sacrifice: Liturgy and Eschatology in Joseph Ratzinger.*

American popular culture is a wasteland when it comes to real life models for a healthy, thriving marriage. Caitrin Bennett believes the most inspiring and helpful examples may well be found among notable Catholic couples from the past. Clearly she's on to something. *Holier Matrimony* should be recommended reading for every couple preparing for marriage and those couples who want to give their marriage new life. Bravo!

In *Holier Matrimony,* Caitrin offers two important challenges. To those preparing for marriage and those looking to re-imagine and strengthen their existing marriage, she offers inspiring, real-life examples of married couples who remained faithful to God and each other in the face of extraordinary adversity. To Church leadership, she offers a challenge to celebrate the role model married Catholic couples offer to a world desperate for examples of faithfulness and commitment.

This book is a treasury of real-life stories about Catholic couples throughout history who suffered enormous hardships yet chose to live a life faithful to God and to their spouse. We meet saints we thought we knew but now see them through the lens of sacred marriage. What we discover are their humanity and their courage. Couples reading this book will come away convinced — "if those couples can do it, so can we."

— **Martin Doblmeier,** Emmy-winning documentary filmmaker (Journey Films).

Each story of married saints contained in this book illuminates a different aspect of the beautiful vocation to marriage. Additionally, the tips and questions for discussion at the end of each chapter help to bring the stories to a practical level. I am grateful for this resource and looking forward to sharing it with married couples and those preparing for Holy Matrimony.

— **Father William Buckley,** priest for the Diocese of Richmond, Virginia.

Christian marriage is no ordinary calling; for two to "become one," to faithfully reflect the union between Christ and His Church, requires not only supernatural aid, but moral support as well! Caitrin Bennett provides just that by connecting us to married saints — whose struggles, sufferings, trials, and triumphs will not fail to encourage and inspire couples seeking to fortify their marriages.

— **Mary Stanford,** theology department, Christendom College, and author of *The Obedience Paradox: Finding True Freedom in Marriage.*

Holier Matrimony by Caitrin Bennett is a must-read for Catholic couples, married or engaged, or anyone who lacks examples of holy marriage in this age that is so fraught with counterfeit love. This book presents the stories of 12 saintly couples who showed the world the beauty and power of God's plan for marriage and family. Readers will discover how these couples faced the joys and sorrows of life with faith, love, and courage. I sobbed through the chapter on Louis and Zélie Martin. The variety of the lives of these holy couples means that all readers will find a saint with whose sufferings they can identify and whose heroic virtue can give them hope to persevere in the bad times and relish the good. The book is great to read on your own but will also be fantastic in a group setting. I hope to use it with my Catholic Moms' book club when it's released. Truly a gem!

— **Samantha Stephenson,** author of *Reclaiming Motherhood from a Culture Gone Mad* and host of the podcast "Brave New Us."

Caitrin Bennett has written an inspiring, informative, and practical book. She uniquely combines instruction on the marital vows, applicable stories from the lives of married saints, and practical advice for combining the two. The result, able to be used to prepare for or improve your marriage, is invaluable. Bennett's approach is comprehensive and clearly rooted in a deep desire to help others see the beauty of the teachings and traditions of the Catholic Church on marriage.

— **Caitlin Lasnoski,** author of *30 Days with Married Saints: A Catholic Couples Devotional.*

Holier Matrimony wonderfully unpacks eight essential vows of marriage by connecting the reader to saintly married role models from the Bible and beyond. Bennett's meticulously researched book sprinkled with reflection questions and beautiful prayers will transform your marriage into a thriving, enduring, and holy covenant.

— **Patrick O'Hearn,** author of *Courtship of the Saints: How the Saints Met their Spouses.*

Holier Matrimony has inspired us to love each other better and helped us gain an even greater appreciation for the graces of this great Sacrament. The married saints that came before us have shown that it is indeed possible to have holier matrimony! Do you want to be encouraged and inspired in your marriage? Read this book. Do you want new friends in Heaven to pray for your marriage? Read this book. Do you want to grow in appreciation for the Sacrament of Holy Matrimony? Read this book. We are so grateful to Caitrin for writing this important book for Catholic married couples!

From the example of married saints to Caitrin's suggestions in each chapter, this book is full of wisdom and tools to help married couples in all stages of life. We pray it inspires a whole new generation of married saints!

— **Jen and Logan Lirette** of SurprisedByMarriage.com.

Build up your marriage with the help of saintly mentors! Caitrin Bennett pairs elements of each marriage vow with stories of saints in this helpful book that's sure to inspire couples at any stage of marriage. A beautiful gift for an engagement, wedding, or anniversary.

— **Barb Szyszkiewicz,** editor at CatholicMom.com and author of *The Handy Little Guide to Prayer.*

I love reading about saints; they give me inspiration and encouragement! So, imagine my joy in finding a book full of holy men and women who share my married vocation! *Holier Matrimony* contains the stories of familiar saints, like Elizabeth and Zachariah and Louis and Zélie Martin, as well as new heavenly friends, like Cyprian and Daphrosa Rugamba and Karl I and Zita of Austria. I would have been happy just reading the thorough summaries Caitrin Bennett recounts of their lives, but then she shares with us so much more: reflection of our marital vows that pair beautifully with each couple, practical ideas on how to live out our promises, and a beautiful prayer to end each chapter. Discussion questions to ponder with one's spouse are an added bonus. And don't skip the Introduction — it provides a great summary of the canonization process and explains the importance of the Communion of Saints. With the example of these married saints, *Holier Matrimony* very well could lead us, by God's good grace, to holier marriages. And with the family under attack as it is today, this book is quite timely.

— **Kelly Guest,** author of *Saintly Moms: 25 Stories of Holiness.*

Caitrin Bennett brings saintly couples fully down-to-earth in these exceptional stories. Inspiring, convicting, and challenging, she will have you desiring, seeking, and cultivating the sacramental grace of a *Holier Matrimony.*

— **Ashley Bateman,** policy writer for The Heartland Institute.

Caitrin draws attention to finding the sacred in the ordinary through her well-researched and relatable writing, with helpful reflection questions and action points throughout. Engaged and married couples will find a beautiful overview of heroic married life as lived by the saints, highlighting the wonderful fact that the universal call to holiness is lived in our unique vocations!

— **Lauren Vitale,** co-founder of Whole Mission Fertility and instructor of the Marquette Method of Natural Family Planning (NFP).

Christian marriage has always been challenging, but today it is under attack as never before. Catholic couples need all the help they can get, especially the example of other couples who have succeeded in living a holy marriage. What better place to look than in the lives of the saints? I have seen personally what a difference Bl. Karl has made in the lives of many couples who have come to know him. Caitrin Bennett has made a great contribution by introducing readers today to some very appealing and holy couples — some already saints, some on the way. She combines an accessible writing style with a unique approach, analyzing the eight distinct promises comprising the traditional Catholic wedding vows, illustrating them with incidents from the lives of her chosen saints, and suggesting thought-provoking questions to help couples today apply these examples to their own lives. I highly recommend this book to husbands and wives and to those preparing for marriage.

— **Suzanne Pearson,** delegate to North America-Emperor Karl League of Prayer.

We all need the witness of the saints to persevere in our vocations. Caitrin brings the stories of these saintly spouses to life, showing us how we, too, can live out heroic virtue in our daily lives, specifically through the lens of the marital vows. This book will be a blessing on anyone currently living out or preparing for holy matrimony.

— **Teresa (Tracy) Kinealy,** author of *Private Devotion,*
Public Action: The Contributions of Madame
Acarie to Post-Reformation French Catholicism
(Master's thesis, University of Oklahoma).

Holier Matrimony is a book that speaks about the universal call to holiness that is not just for the religious or clergy, but for everyone including married couples. Caitrin Bennett introduces us to several married saints who challenge spouses to image God's love through their lives. Those who are called to this vocation are given concrete examples in the book on how to live the message of love even with trials and suffering. Her selection of saints shows that love is not just a feeling but a decision to make a total gift of self, and that it requires sacrifice and holiness.

— **Kathy Schmugge,** senior director of the Secretariat
of Discipleship and director of Family Life,
Diocese of Charleston, South Carolina.

HOLIER MATRIMONY

Married Saints, Catholic Vows,
and Sacramental Grace

Caitrin Bennett

Available from:
Marian Helpers Center
Stockbridge, MA 01263
Prayerline: 1-800-804-3823
Orderline: 1-800-462-7426

Websites:
ShopMercy.org
TheDivineMercy.org

Library of Congress Catalog Number: 2024942585
ISBN: 978-1-59614-629-7

Imprimi Potest:
Very Rev. Chris Alar, MIC
Provincial Superior
The Blessed Virgin Mary, Mother of Mercy Province
July 26, 2024
Feast of Saints Joachim and Anne, Parents of the Blessed Virgin Mary

Nihil Obstat:
Robert A. Stackpole, STD
Censor Deputatus
July 26, 2024

Note: The *Nihil Obstat* and corresponding *Imprimi Potest* are not a certification that those granting it agree with the contents, opinions, or statements expressed in the work. Instead, they merely confirm that the work contains nothing contrary to faith and morals.

Layout and Cover Design: Kathy Szpak

All images are public domain, except for those supplied on pages 14 and 121 and published with permission.

Scripture texts in this work are taken from the New American Bible, revised edition © 2010, 1991, 1986, 1970 Confraternity of Christian Doctrine, Washington, DC, and are used by permission of the copyright owner. All Rights Reserved. No part of the New American Bible may be reproduced in any form without permission in writing from the copyright owner.

Excerpts from the English translation of the *Catechism of the Catholic Church* for use in the United States of America Copyright © 1994, United States Catholic Conference, Inc. — Libreria Editrice Vaticana. Used with Permission. English translation of the *Catechism of the Catholic Church*: Modifications from the Editio Typica copyright © 1997, United States Conference of Catholic Bishops — Libreria Editrice Vaticana.

To my husband Chris —
my vocation and my helpmate.

TABLE OF CONTENTS

The Catholic Marital Vows

From "The Order of Celebrating Matrimony," #60,[1] as presented at the wedding ceremony of Christopher and Caitrin Bennett on April 16, 2016, before Fr. Tom Ferguson in Good Shepherd Catholic Church in Alexandria, Virginia.

"Christopher and Caitrin, have you come here to enter into marriage without coercion, freely and wholeheartedly (fully)?

"Are you prepared, as you follow the path of marriage, to love and honor each other for as long as you both shall live (faithfully)?

"Are you prepared to accept children lovingly from God and to bring them up according to the law of Christ and His Church (fruitfully)?"

"We are."

"Since it is your intention to enter into the covenant of holy matrimony, join your right hands, and declare your consent before God and his Church."

"I, Christopher, take you, Caitrin, for my lawful wife, to have and to hold, from this day forward...for better, for worse...for richer, for poorer...in sickness and in health...until death do us part."

"I, Caitrin, take you, Christopher, for my lawful husband, to have and to hold, from this day forward...for better, for worse...for richer, for poorer...in sickness and in health...until death do us part."

PREFACE

Your Marriage Needs this Book

Modern American couples are postponing marriage more than ever before — if they get married at all. So many have lost faith in matrimony that the year 2020 saw 28% fewer marriages as compared to the year 2000, despite overall population growth of 17% during that time.[1] For those who do marry, more than one in three will be divorced at least once.[2]

The current climate surrounding marriage can make engaged and newlywed couples feel disheartened or even hopeless. But what if the cure for this modern problem is waiting to be rediscovered within one of the world's oldest institutions?

The Catholic Church offers beautiful and valuable gifts to those who seek Heaven via the vocational path of marriage. The Catholic marital vows, found on a previous page of this book, form a comprehensive "job description" for a holy spouse. Married saints who have already made it to Heaven serve as inspiration and excellent role-models to those of us in the trenches. Most importantly, by means of the grace communicated in a sacramental marriage, Jesus Himself empowers spouses to love as He loves.

If you are an engaged or married Catholic thirsting for *holier* matrimony than you so often observe, you have come to the right place. This book will help you unwrap and tap into the power of the gifts Jesus has given us through His Church. As you read, you will grow in understanding of your marriage vows, and, more importantly, you will become better equipped to live them out. You will befriend several married saints who also lived out these vows, reflect on how you can emulate their lives and marriages, and ask for their intercession. You will learn to strive constantly towards holiness, and to rely on that most precious gift of marital grace when you and your spouse inevitably fall short.

As married Christians, our ultimate goal is to get ourselves, our spouses, and our children to Heaven. This would be impossible for us to accomplish on our own. But Jesus has given us everything we need: His Church to teach us, His saints to inspire us, and His grace to empower us. Together, let's unwrap these gifts and begin our journey towards *Holier Matrimony.*

Introduction

Before we begin this journey, we need to cover a bit of background information. I want to make sure you understand the concept of sainthood before we meet our married saints. We will discuss the vows of our marriage covenant throughout the book, so this is also a good time to explain what a covenant is and how central it is to the Christian faith. Finally, I will explain how this book is organized and show you how to make the most of every page.

Who Are the Saints?

Saints are holy people who have died and are now in Heaven with God. Saints come from all corners of the world, from the Vietnamese martyrs who were brutally tortured for their faith, to St. Juan Diego, an indigenous Mexican who witnessed the famous apparition of Our Lady of Guadalupe. Some saints lived during Jesus' lifetime, like St. Veronica who wiped His bloody face, and St. John the Apostle and Evangelist. We are also blessed with much more recent saints, like St. Maximilian Kolbe, who gave his life for another at Auschwitz, and the well-loved St. "Mother" Teresa of Calcutta.

During their lives on earth, some saints were wealthy and powerful, some were extremely poor; some wrote brilliant theological doctrines, while others were illiterate. Many were priests, religious sisters or brothers, but some were married — and you will meet a few in this book!

The Church bestows the title of "saint" on people whose lives have been scrutinized carefully through a long process called canonization. Throughout this book, we will meet not only full-fledged saints, but also several holy men and women whose canonization process is not yet complete. Some are Servants of God (SoG), whose local bishop has recognized their lives of holiness and received approval from the Vatican to collect evidence for their cause; others are Venerables (Ven.), whose causes have been approved for opening by a Vatican-appointed council; and a few are Blesseds (Bl.), meaning that one verified miracle has already been attributed to that person's intercession. A second such miracle is required to complete the process of canonization and declare the individual a Saint (St.).[1]

Finding *Your* Saints

The actual number of fully canonized Saints is hard to determine, but the consensus seems to be at least 800. Add in the Servants of God, Venerables, and Blesseds, and the list of saints can become overwhelming. It would be great to learn about all these men and women, but there are simply too many to get through. Where should we even start?

One method is to seek out saints who are like us in some way. Maybe, as a Latina, you relate to St. Rose of Lima, Peru. Maybe you love to play soccer, and you find an example in St. Luigi Scrosoppi, the sport's patron saint. You might even feel a connection with a saint because you share his or her name. (No luck for me there — I'm hoping to be the original St. Caitrin!) All saints are valuable teachers, but it is often easiest to learn from a teacher to whom you can easily relate. We recognize ourselves in them and see a flicker of promise in their path to Heaven. *If she can do it, maybe I can, too.*

For my part, I loved reading about the boldness of young St. Joan of Arc when I was a teenager. I've also prayed for the intercession of St. Joseph of Cupertino, the patron saint of students and test-takers, before a big college exam, and I can't count the number of times I have called upon St. Anthony of Padua to "come around" when something was lost and needed to be found. But when I got married a few years ago, I suddenly realized … *none* of my go-to saints were married.

Where Are All the Married Saints?

Through the ages, a huge majority of Catholics lived out a vocation to marriage, not the religious life. Shouldn't there be many more married saints than religious? The answer is that there probably are! What we lack are not married saints but *canonized* married saints. You see, Heaven is likely teeming with the souls of holy men and women who were married during their earthly lives, and those are all, by definition, saints. However, through the ages, the Church has been much less likely to have officially canonized a married person than a priest or religious person. There are a handful of reasons for this.

First, married people are oriented inwards, towards their families, while most other vocations are oriented *"ad extra,"* outside of themselves, to pray for or serve society at large. This means that family life, however holy, can often go unnoticed. It is also important to note that almost all people canonized for many centuries were either martyrs or religious. Through the dying-to-self of monasticism, or the actual dying of martyrdom, these saints were seen as already following what Fr. David Callum of *Catholic Insight* calls the "angelic life." Canonization, he says, was "simply the recognition of what had been achieved."[2] Family life is not monastic, and married people also generally tend to avoid being martyred so they can continue to care for their families.

Finally, it takes a lot of lobbying to pursue a canonization effort at all, and even more to keep pushing through the long and often tedious process. Members of a religious order have both the helpful connections and the strong motive to lobby for the canonization of one of their own. A beloved priest's hundreds or thousands of parishioners can all work together to have him recognized for saintly virtue.[3] But here, once again, married people are at a disadvantage for being canonized.

There are still far more religious people canonized than lay people today, but the Church has been canonizing more lay people in the past century or so than ever before. By the way, this also includes some non-married lay people, like St. Giuseppe Moscati, a noted Italian doctor and scientific researcher who was canonized by Pope St. John Paul II. Among married saints, we have watched the first couple beatified together, the Quattrocchis (featured in chapter 4), as well as the first couple fully canonized together, the Martins (find them in chapter 1), in just the past 25 years!

In researching this book, I looked through long lists of saints to find those precious few who took — and stuck to — the same vows that I took on my wedding day. Not the vows of chastity, poverty, and obedience taken by clergy and religious, but instead vows of *free, full, faithful,* and *fruitful* love to my spouse; *for better or for worse, for richer or for poorer, in sickness and in health, until death do us part.* These are the vows of our marriage covenant.

Covenants

What do I mean when I say that marriage is a "covenant"? A covenant is a holy, unbreakable contract. In Hebrew, the word for covenant is *b'rith,* which is better translated as a "family bond."[4] Throughout the Bible, God seeks to bind His people — His family — to Himself through covenants. In the book of Genesis alone, God makes covenants with Adam, Noah, and Abraham. What is more, God is faithful to His covenants even when His people break them. For example, God kept His promise to Noah that He would never again flood the earth, though people began to sin against Him soon after the Flood. God sealed this covenant of protection for His people with a beautiful rainbow, and He continues to send us the same sign today as a reminder of His faithfulness after storms (see Gen 9).

God promised Abraham and, later, David that He would bless the world through their lineage. He told them that they would be His chosen people even when they did not claim Him as their only God. This covenant, sealed in flesh through circumcision, was fulfilled in Abraham and David's descendant, Jesus Christ, the Savior of the world.

Finally, the New Covenant made in Jesus' Blood is the most beautiful one of all. Not only will God protect us from His wrath, not only will He bless us and call us His people, but in Christ we are promised a *close, personal relationship* with the God of the universe (see Jn. 15:15). We are finally brought up into the family that is our triune God: Father, Son, and Holy Spirit. We have seen that "only God keeps His covenant promises."[5] But this time, the covenant will be everlasting and unbroken, because Jesus, both man and God, made it Himself on behalf of the whole human race.

God communes intimately with His covenant people through the Sacraments of His Church. For example, God marks us as His own and brings us into His family through Baptism. He forgives our sins in Confession so that we can turn back to Him and restore our wounded relationship. Every time we receive the Eucharist, we experience the greatest intimacy of all, as Christ gives Himself to us, Body, Blood, Soul, and Divinity.

Marriage: Sacrament and Covenant

The Sacrament of Holy Matrimony is itself a holy contract, a family bond, and a covenant witnessed by God. In fact, "the covenant between the spouses is integrated into God's covenant with man."[6] We learn how to be faithful to our covenant by reading about God's faithfulness to His. Not only that, but when we are weak, God Himself gives us the strength to be faithful to our vows.

Like all Sacraments, the Sacrament of Holy Matrimony both "signifies and communicates grace,"[7] which is the help of God. The specific graces communicated in marriage give us supernatural strength to successfully uphold our covenant. As the *Catechism of the Catholic Church* puts it, the Holy Spirit becomes "the ever-available source of [our] love and the strength to renew [our] fidelity."[8]

This is encouraging news for anyone who has ever doubted whether they married the perfect person. We don't hope we will find our "soulmate" by chance, but instead trust that the sacramental grace of marriage will bolster us when the going gets tough. "Choose a man who loves God and loves you like Christ loves the Church," a spiritual role-model once told me, "and on that altar, he will *become* your soulmate."

To strengthen our marriage covenant, we must learn the vows of that covenant. We didn't walk down the aisle to promise our spouse that we wouldn't flood the earth again, and we didn't take the same vows as religious brothers, sisters, and priests, either. We took vows to love our spouse freely, fully, faithfully, and fruitfully; for better or for worse, for richer or for poorer, in sickness and in health, until death do us part.

When we spoke those vows, did we truly understand what we were promising? For example, what does it mean to love fruitfully? What are some concrete ways to show your spouse that you love him or her for richer or for poorer? Read on and you will find out!

How to Use this Book

Each chapter of this book is organized in the same way. First, you will read the brief biography of a married saint or saintly couple. Following this is a discussion of one marital vow I thought was especially exemplified in their biography, with practical ways you can live it out in your own marriage. I include a prayer that is connected to the saint(s) and/or the target vow for that chapter, and then leave you with a few questions to ponder and discuss after reading.

Here are some quick tips to help you make the most of each of these four chapter elements.

As you read the biography that makes up the largest portion of each chapter, picture yourself meeting a new friend. You will hear the story of their lives, marriages, and journeys of faith, often in their own words. Try to find connections between yourself and your new holy friend — a shared interest in music, a common struggle with anger. Note the daily habits of the saints we meet: when and how they prayed, how they addressed their spouse and children, what they did with their time. These small, quotidian habits often formed these saints' paths to Heaven, and you can easily adopt some into your own daily routine.

Next, you will come to the section regarding that chapter's target marriage vow. First, think back on the biography you just finished reading and track that vow through the saint's life. Did they ever struggle with this vow? If so, how did they grow in understanding of the vow, and what choices followed? After this warm-up, take the time to track this same vow throughout your own life and marriage so far, considering how you also might live out the vow more deeply. These sections on the vows also offer practical suggestions to get you started.

This is the time to highlight, underline, or jot some ideas in the margins. I give you full permission to <u>use</u> this book!

Each chapter's prayer can be found towards the end. You might come back to one of these prayers when you are struggling with a particular marital vow or seeking the intercession of a particular married saint. These prayers can also be a good way to open a discussion with your spouse after you have both read the preceding biography and vow sections. Pray together, share your notes and initial thoughts, then tackle the discussion questions that close the chapter. Small groups of couples in marriage preparation or enrichment programs could also structure discussion around these sections.

Keeping these suggestions in mind will help you make the most of this book. Guided by some of history's holiest married people and two thousand years of beautiful Church teaching, your marriage can be truly transformed into a thriving "community of life and love,"[9] as Pope St. John Paul II encouraged.

Let's get started!

CHAPTER 1

Loving Freely:
SAINTS LOUIS AND ZÉLIE MARTIN

FEAST DAY: JULY 12

The first thing the priest asks a couple on their wedding day is whether they have come freely to the Sacrament. If one or both spouses is coerced into marriage, their union would not be valid. This concept stretches far past the wedding, as the couple continues to freely choose to love one another each day. In this chapter, we will discuss cutting ourselves free from sin, anxiety, and worldliness to achieve self-mastery. The freer you are, the more freely you can love.

Saints Louis and Zélie Martin are great examples of living this vow. "Set free from the slavery that sin represents," a biographer explained, "the Martins were free to love and didn't deprive themselves of love."[1]

They shared this love with their five daughters, all of whom grew up to become holy nuns. The youngest was the beloved St. Thérèse of Lisieux, who wrote, "The good Lord has given me a father and a mother who are more worthy of Heaven than of earth!"[2] Let's meet the couple that raised one of the greatest saints of our time, particularly noting how they lived out their vow to love one another freely.

Louis and Zélie's Childhoods

Louis Martin was born in Bordeaux, France, on Aug. 22, 1823. As a child, he was inspired by the vibrant faith of his parents, Captain Pierre-François and Marie-Anne "Fanny" Martin. After Louis, two Martin daughters survived childhood: Marie-Anne and Anne-Françoise-Fanny Martin.

Louis spent most of his childhood in Alençon. Though he did not attend secondary school, Louis was very intelligent and had a passion for French literature. He also showed talent from a young age for drawing and painting, and had an appreciation for beauty. Louis was an interesting mix: a "tender man of depth focused on God," who was also known to break up knife fights and volunteer as a firefighter. This mixture of qualities was even evident in Louis' appearance: "[T]all ... with the bearing of an officer," but with "soft, deep light in his hazel eyes. He looked like both a gentleman and a mystic."[3]

Azélie-Marie Guérin, always known just as Zélie, was born to Isidore and Louise-Jeanne Guérin on Dec. 23, 1831, just outside Alençon in Gandelain. Her father served in the army before switching to police work. Zélie had two siblings, with whom she remained close throughout her life. Elder sister Marie-Louise ("Elise") was Zélie's best friend and spiritual role-model, especially after Elise became Sr. Marie-Dosithée at the Visitation Convent. Her brother Isidore was much younger, and Zélie loved him, "as a mother would."[4]

Despite good relationships with her siblings, Zélie did not have the happiest childhood. The Guérin family was poor, occasionally struggling to make ends meet. Zélie was often ill, tormented with migraine headaches from about age seven to 12. She later wrote that she also "suffered a lot" from the severe treatment of her mother.[5] Even as an adult, she struggled with dark thoughts and a "melancholic" edge to her temperament. Somehow, little Zélie still managed to do brilliantly in school and to maintain a deep faith in God, a devotion to Our Lady, and a "restless ... eagerness for work."[6]

Young Adulthood

As young adults, both Louis and Zélie desired to pursue vocations to the religious life. At 23, Louis left his apprenticeship as a watchmaker and presented himself to the monks at the famous monastery of St. Bernard's. The monks there split their lives between contemplation and rescuing people lost in the deep snow of the Alps, and this seemed the perfect fit for Louis' meditative but adventurous soul. The superiors were eager to have him, too, until they learned that Louis had never studied Latin. Louis began studying Latin, but when illness interrupted his studies, he felt it was a sign. He chose to pursue a "quasi-monastic life in the world"[7] instead of in the monastery.

Zélie, meanwhile, had been attracted to the religious life since her days of learning from nuns at school. She was brokenhearted to be rejected by the Daughters of Charity when she was 19, possibly because of her poor health. While Louis rejected the idea of marriage and expected to remain single, Zélie assumed she was meant to marry if she had no vocation to the religious life. She prayed to God, "I beg Thee ... to send me many children, and grant that they may all be consecrated to Thee!"[8]

After eight total years of study and apprenticeship, Louis set up his own watch shop in Alençon in 1850. The business was so successful that he soon added a jewelry store to the establishment. Louis lived with his parents and spent his time reading, fishing, and gardening at his "Pavilion," land he purchased on the outskirts of town. He was also very involved with the Catholic Circle, a group of friends that prayed, did acts of charity, and played billiards together.

Meanwhile, Zélie had found her own craft to pursue. In 1853, she heard an inner voice calling her to learn the art of lacemaking, for which the town of Alençon was particularly known. She and her sister "started working the very next day," and their business took off quickly.[9] A few years later, Zélie met her future mother-in-law, Fanny Martin, at a lace-making class.

Meeting and Marriage

Zélie first passed Louis on the Saint-Léonard Bridge, and again heard an inner voice. "This is the one I have prepared for you," the voice told her.[10] Just a few days later, Fanny formally introduced her son to Zélie. Their "spiritual harmony established itself so quickly" that they were married three months later. [11] Father Hurel, leader of Louis' Catholic Circle, celebrated their union on July 13, 1858. The wedding occurred at midnight, "shrouded in intimacy and prayer."[12] Louis was 34 and Zélie, 26.

According to their daughter, the two had "[d]ifferent temperaments, but perfectly well-matched, each one completing ... the deficiencies of the other."[13] When Zélie overworked herself or felt weighed down by worry, Louis' cheerful disposition lifted her back up. When Louis delved too deeply into meditation and abstract thought, Zélie brought him back down to earth. Each was also truly grateful to have the companionship and encouragement of the other. Zélie, who was a prolific letter writer, wrote of Louis in 1863, "[He] makes my life sweet. He is truly my holy husband; I would wish a husband like him for every woman."[14] Louis signed his letters to Zélie, "Your husband and true friend, who loves you for life."[15]

One might be surprised to hear that such a romantic couple started their union with ten months of celibacy. Apparently, Zélie had no understanding of sexuality at the time of her marriage, and Louis had to explain "the birds and the bees" to his wife. She went to see her sister at the convent that day, and claimed she cried more than she ever did in her life. "I felt so unhappy seeing myself living in the midst of the world," she later wrote. "I wanted to live a hidden life, to hide my life alongside hers."[16] Louis was more than understanding, as he, too, had once desired to live a secluded life at St. Bernard's. The couple agreed to have a "Josephite marriage," imitating the Blessed Virgin and St. Joseph by never consummating their marriage. During this time, they fostered a boy who had ten siblings and whose mother had died. Between this experience and the advice of a spiritual director, Zélie and Louis were eventually persuaded to have children, but they did not regret these celibate months. "I believe our mutual affection was even more increased through this,"[17] Zélie wrote. They learned to show their love for one another in other ways, and they became more united spiritually.

Parenthood

Skeptical at first about the sexual aspect of marriage, the Martins soon found that they could become holy through parenthood. Something new clicked into place when their eldest child, Marie, was born. Louis eagerly told his priest, "This is the first time you've seen me here for a baptism, but it won't be the last!"[18]

The Martin girls seemed to come in pairs. "Nonconformist" Marie and "sympathetic and lively" Pauline were the eldest, born in 1860 and 1861. These two would serve as little mothers to the other children. Léonie, the most difficult child, and her counterpart, the "great beauty" Hélène, were born in 1863 and 1864. After the very early deaths of two sons and a daughter, there remained the youngest pair. "Sensitive, intelligent" Céline was born in 1869, and, finally, Louis' "little queen," Thérèse, completed the family in 1873.[19]

Zélie "tolerated neither self-will nor childish whims" as a mother. "[S]he was strict to a certain extent,"[20] but her aim was always to raise holy children by keeping them away from worldly attachments. Still, Zélie worked hard to give her daughters the warmth and tender love she had not received from her own mother. "Ah! How delicate a Mother's heart really is, and how it shows its tenderness in a thousand little cares that no one else thinks about!"[21] Specifically, Thérèse remembered that she would call for her Mama at each step of the staircase, "not moving from there until she heard the voice saying, 'Yes, my little child!'" Thérèse would one day teach the novices in the convent to call for God at each step of their spiritual life, too.[22]

Louis was a just, upright father who served as a wonderful example to his daughters. He devoted a section of the garden at his Pavilion to each child, and loved to take them out on walks or to fish. In the evenings, after family prayer, he sang to them in his beautiful voice. "I cannot say how much I loved Papa," Thérèse shared. "Everything in him caused me to admire him."[23] She had many fond early memories of her "dear king" letting her sit on his boot as he walked around the family's property.

Business Owners

Besides being parents, Louis and Zélie were busy running both their watchmaking and lacemaking businesses from 1858 – 1870. In the end, it became clear that lacemaking was more profitable, so Louis sold his watchmaking shop to his nephew. "It was no small thing ... for a husband to leave his own professional work to devote himself to his wife's endeavors,"[24] but Louis was not bound by pride. In this way he also showed his freedom.

Business boomed. Zélie delegated work to as many as 15 women, while Louis did the bookkeeping and frequently travelled to make deliveries. On their busiest days, the couple worked from 4:30 a.m. to 11:00 p.m. This load could have been alleviated by doing some work on Sundays, but the Martins refused outright to work on the Lord's Day. Instead, Sundays were for Mass, Adoration, family time, Louis' reading, and Zélie's correspondence.

Habits of Faith

Each spouse had his or her own habits of faith. Louis loved to go on pilgrimages to places like Chartres, and he found God both on long nature walks and in the Adoration chapel late at night. Zélie was more of a homebody, preferring to pray novenas with her daughters, especially to the Sacred Heart or to St. Joseph. She was a Third Order Franciscan, which brought her "joyful freedom" that helped her "detach from ... rigidity"[25] that she was otherwise prone to in her spiritual life. They both went to Confession regularly, and they were passionate about helping people in their community receive the Last Rites before death.

The whole family also shared a devotion to the Blessed Mother. They all wore scapulars throughout their lives. A large statue of Mary in their garden became known as "Our Lady of the Smile" when Thérèse was miraculously cured after a smile from it. The children adorned the statue with flowers, especially during the month of May, which is dedicated to Mary. At one point the statue's fingers had to be replaced from being kissed and held so often![26]

Enduring Loss

Life was not always so pleasant for the Martins. After welcoming four healthy daughters, they lost two sons, Joseph-Louis and Joseph-Jean-Baptiste, in 1867 and 1868. Neither survived to his first birthday. Zélie's father, who was living with the Martins, died ten days after Joseph-Jean-Baptiste. Zélie was grieved to the point of physical illness after these deaths. "Someone would have to walk that path to know what torment really is," she wrote. "I do not know if purgatory is worse than this."[27]

Possibly most painful of all was the sudden loss of the beautiful Hélène, who was five years old. What appeared to be a typical illness worsened quickly, and she died unexpectedly with her head on Zélie's shoulder. When Louis "saw his little girl had died, he began sobbing and crying out, 'My little Hélène! My little Hélène!'" Once they had calmed down slightly, Zélie wrote, "Together we offered her to God." Zélie dressed her daughter and put her in the casket herself. "I thought I would die doing it, but I did not want others touching her," she explained. "I will grieve all my life over little Hélène!"[28]

After Hélène's death, the family lost one more daughter, Mélanie-Thérèse, under especially tragic circumstances. For medical reasons, Zélie relied on wet nurses to feed most of her children. The family's trusted wet nurse, Rose Taillé, was unavailable at the time of Mélanie-Thérèse's birth, and the replacement wet nurse was inattentive. Poor Mélanie died of malnutrition. Her death in the fall of 1870 was the fifth loss for the family in less than four years. When "little Thérèse" (as she was the second Thérèse) seemed close to death in her early days, Zélie begged St. Joseph to save her child, unable to imagine losing yet another baby. Rose Taillé stepped in, and Thérèse grew healthily in the Taillé home.

Louis and Zélie somehow endured all these tragedies with incredible hope in God. In her weakest moments, Zélie wrote that she was being "sustained from on high,"[29] comforted by the idea that her children were happy in Heaven and interceding for her family. These intercessory prayers proved efficacious right away: just five days after their first son had died, his sister was miraculously cured of a nasty ear infection. Thérèse wrote much later, "[M]y devotion for my little brothers and sisters has grown and I love to hold dialogues with them frequently."[30]

With God's grace, Louis and Zélie had found some silver linings to the dark clouds, and they looked forward to meeting their children again in Heaven. Still, the pain would never leave them in this life. When her sister-in-law Céline lost a child, Zélie wrote to her, "[I]t is a great good to have a child in heaven, but it is not less painful for our human nature to lose the child; these are the great sorrows of our lives."[31]

Other Trials

Sadly, these deaths were not the only trials facing the Martins in those years. In late 1870, the family had to take refuge in the cellar from the bombardment as the Prussians invaded Alençon. They were subsequently forced to quarter nine German soldiers in their home. Louis lodged a complaint when one of these soldiers stole a watch from him. Upon hearing that looters were being killed for their crimes, though, he withdrew the charge. Louis found that such trying circumstances actually helped him learn to control his temper, and Zélie saw God working to free her from material attachments during the war years. "We will learn to live with less,"[32] she asserted after the town's invasion.

Meanwhile, the Martins' third daughter Léonie's obstinate "backward" character was also becoming a difficulty for her parents. Though her aunt at the Visitation Monastery was convinced Léonie would eventually become a saint, the nuns there were unable to keep instructing her due to her lack of control and "unruliness."[33] Zélie was deeply concerned for her daughter. "I could lose my mind over this," she once wrote.[34]

Slowly, though, Louis and Zélie became aware of the roots of Léonie's temperament. She was probably traumatized at a young age when her "pair" Hélène died. Marie and Pauline were very close, as were Céline and Thérèse, but Léonie was the odd one out. Kicked out of the convent where her older sisters studied with their aunt, Léonie was sent to study with two "nuns" who ended up not being true nuns at all, and who were abusive to the other girl they had taken in. Thus, this second option for Léonie's education also fell through traumatically. At home, meanwhile, Léonie herself was being constantly mistreated and "terrified" by a family servant, Louise. It was no wonder she had trouble trusting adults at this point, even her saintly parents.

Before her aunt's passing, Léonie had written her these words: "When you get to Heaven, will you please ask ... God ... to give me the grace to be converted and ... the vocation of becoming a true religious."[35] The very next month, the Martins finally learned about the maid who was abusing Léonie and were able to reestablish trust with their daughter. Léonie and Zélie both attributed this to the intercession of Zélie's sister in Heaven. And Aunt Marie Dosithée may have been right about "turbulent" Léonie becoming a saint after all. After several tries, Léonie would eventually become a nun at her aunt's convent, and in 2015 Léonie's own beatification case was opened! She may one day be the fourth canonized saint from the Martin family.

Zélie's Illness

It was good timing for Zélie to repair her relationship with Léonie, because she didn't have much time left. In late 1876, Zélie was diagnosed with malignant breast cancer. Her doctor informed her that there was nothing to be done. She was as accepting of God's will as ever. "[L]et us not worry about it; it will always be whatever God wants," she wrote. Her only concern was for her children, especially wayward Léonie and four-year-old Thérèse. "Ah, if it wasn't for them," she shared, "death would not frighten me."[36]

Louis had a much more difficult time accepting God's will in this matter, however. "My husband cannot be comforted.

He stopped his fishing ... he doesn't go to our circle of friends anymore. He's devastated,"[37] Zélie wrote. At his insistence, she agreed to take a pilgrimage to Lourdes to seek miraculous healing, but internally she was truly making the pilgrimage for her children's health. After visiting the pools of Lourdes, Zélie felt that Our Lady had the same message for Zélie that she had given St. Bernadette: "I will make you all happy, not in this world but in the next."[38] Zélie knew she would not be healed of her cancer.

By July, Zélie could not "dress or undress [her]self alone," but she kept going to Mass and Communion as long as she possibly could with her husband's help. Louis attended to her carefully at home and would even "take [her] in his arms like a child." On Aug. 26, he arranged for his wife to receive the last rites, as he had done for countless other community members over the years. After this, Zélie "suffered less," though she was paralyzed.[39]

At age 46 and after 19 years of marriage, Zélie Martin died on Aug. 28, 1877. Thérèse remembers kneeling by her mother's bed with her four sisters and seeing her father "sobbing."[40] After Zélie's death, local priests "declared openly that there was one more saint now in Heaven."[41]

Louis Picks Up the Pieces

To focus on his daughters' upbringing, Louis closed his business. He also decided to move the family to Lisieux to be near Isidore and Céline Guérin, at great sacrifice. Louis' mother, his friends, his Pavilion, and the gravesites of his beloved wife and children were all in Alençon, but he knew relocation was the best decision for his daughters. Louis left his mother in the care of (who else?) dear Rose Taillé and purchased a villa in Lisieux called *Les Buissonnets* ("little bushes").

Louis did not create a social circle for himself in Lisieux as he had in Alençon. He spent his time reading, praying, and caring for his daughters. Generally, he only left the house for two reasons: to take long afternoon walks in the countryside, often with his "little Queen," and to attend 6:00 a.m. Mass with his older daughters. Why so early? "It's the only Mass,"

Louis said, "that the women in service jobs and the blue-collar men can go to. At this Mass we are together with the poor."[42]

Because of Louis' constant example, Thérèse affirmed, "the practice of virtue became sweet and natural to us." He always prioritized family time and, above all, family prayer. The girls had "only to look at him to see how the saints pray." Louis was more concerned with Heaven than with earthly things, and his daughters learned to free themselves of the world in turn. Though Thérèse described their years at *Les Buissonnets* as "the ideal of happiness," she and her sisters were all ready to "turn away from it freely" when God called them to religious life.[43]

Called to Carmelite Life

In 1882, Pauline became the first daughter to become a Carmelite nun. Marie followed in 1886. In truth, the older sisters had put off their vocation for several years to help care for the younger girls. In 1887, little Thérèse announced that she, too, was called to Carmel. However, she was turned away because she was only 14. Louis was deeply saddened at the idea of losing a third daughter so quickly, but he promised to help Thérèse become a Carmelite sister despite her age. Little did he know that they would have to go to Rome to seek permission from the Pope himself! To Thérèse's joy, their journey was successful, and in 1888, she became a postulant at the Lisieux Carmel.

The following day Louis wrote, "Thérèse, my little queen, entered Carmel yesterday. God alone can exact such a sacrifice, but he helps me mightily so that in the midst of my tears my heart overflows with joy."[44] Many friends described Louis as a "modern Abraham,"[45] offering his daughters to the Lord just as Abraham was willing to offer his son, Isaac (see Gen 22:1-9). "The Lord ... has paid me [a great honor] in choosing all [my] daughters ...to be his brides," Louis later told Céline. "If I had anything better, I would not hesitate to offer it to him."[46]

Louis in a Mental Institution

Thérèse had heard Louis say that he was too happy in life and wanted to face some trial. God must have heard his prayer, because in 1887, Louis experienced several strokes, episodes of paralysis, hemorrhaging, memory loss, and depression. By 1888, he was hallucinating frequently and would sometimes wander off and disappear for days. Isidore Guérin made the tough decision to send his brother-in-law to the *Bon Sauveur* Asylum in Caen for his own safety.

Mental institutions of the day were dark places. Still, Louis was able to bring many fellow patients to God during his time at the asylum. He also believed that his illness and humiliation there constituted the trials he had sought in order to prepare himself for Heaven.

In 1892, Louis was able to return home to his two remaining daughters. Léonie left for the convent the following year; Céline also felt called there but chose to stay with Louis so long as he needed her. "Papa had become my little child," she wrote to her sisters in the Carmel.[47]

Louis was hardly able to speak when he visited his daughters at Carmel for the last time. He simply pointed up and whispered, "In Heaven!" They knew what he meant. When he died on July 28, 1894, at age 71, Thérèse pictured Louis reunited with Zélie and the children who had died too young. "The two stems [Louis and Zélie] who brought these flowers into existence are now reunited for all eternity," she rejoiced. When their remaining five children died, the beautiful "lily plant" of the Martin family would be "complete in Heaven."[48]

The Martins' Canonization and Patronage

Thérèse's canonization just 28 years after her death sparked interest in the parents who raised her. Two separate cases were then opened to canonize Louis and Zélie, but the cases were joined in 1971. It had become obvious that the Martins' journeys of holiness were indivisible. Together, they were declared Venerables in 1994, Blesseds in 2008, and finally Saints in 2015. They were the first married couple ever canonized together.

The Martins' beatification and canonization miracles both involved the healing of infants, which shows how often parents seek the intercession of this couple. People everywhere striving to raise little saints have befriended Sts. Louis and Zélie. We seek their intercession and note their example, "struck by their vitality, their modernity, and their dynamism"[49] as married people, parents, business owners, and Catholic Christians.

Marital Vow: Loving Freely

Loving freely requires being free to love. You must be master of yourself, not bound by anxiety, materialism, sin, or addiction. Jesus proved that He was Master of Himself throughout the temptations of Satan. Then, He told His followers, "I lay down my life in order to take it up again" (Jn 10:17). Jesus was free to choose, and He chose to lay down His life out of love for His sheep.

As young adults, Louis and Zélie Martin hoped to free themselves from worldly attachments and concerns through cloistered religious life. Instead, God called them (as He calls so many of us!) to be "in the world but not of the world" as married people. Their success is evident in these words Thérèse wrote of her father: "The things of earth seemed hardly to touch him."[50]

What attitudes and habits rendered Sts. Louis and Zélie so free of unhealthy attachments? How can we grow in freedom so that we may love our own spouses more freely?

Fear and Anxiety

Fear and anxiety can consume the mind, leaving a person unable to trust God or others. Zélie confessed that she used to worry about all the details of her lace-making business, even feeling convinced at times that the entire business was on the brink of collapse. When she finally let go and entrusted those worries to God, she felt liberated.

It is also liberating to be able to trust your spouse. When Zélie was preparing for her death, she had to trust that Louis would care for their young children. "Love trusts, it sets free,

it does not try to control, possess and dominate everything."[51]
If you track every move your spouse makes, or if your spouse
is constantly watching you, something in the relationship is
broken and needs healing.

Some ways to free yourself from the bonds of anxiety:

- Pray the Surrender Novena (available online) to entrust
  all your worries to God.

- If possible, take something off your plate so you can
  focus more time and energy on your spiritual life and
  your marriage.

- Talk through concerns and uncertainties with your
  spouse frequently, trying to be nonjudgmental to
  improve communication.

- Try a simple prayer like this one: "God, by the grace
  of my marriage, empower me to trust my spouse more
  today."

Materialism and Worldly Comfort

In our consumer society, many people are slaves to materialism,
pride, and envy. Because their business was so successful, the
Martins could have lived a fairly luxurious lifestyle. However,
they actively rejected "slavery to fashion" and "shunned excess"[52]
by purchasing simple clothing, furniture, and food. Zélie's sister
wrote that their prosperity did not make the Martins proud, but
instead convinced them to give more generously to the needy.[53]

To break their attachments to creature comforts, the
Martins practiced small sacrifices. For example, Louis forbade
himself from "crossing his legs, drinking between meals, and
drawing closer to the fire."[54] There is nothing morally wrong
with moving closer to the fire when you're cold. Louis simply
chose to deny himself a few arbitrary comforts so that he could
gain mastery over himself and be ready to say "no" to much
bigger temptations in life. You will see similar practices in the
lives of all the other saintly people we will meet in this book.
Like little Thérèse, the saints all knew "[i]t is so easy to go astray
on the flowery paths of the world"[55] if they indulged their every
desire for comfort and satisfaction.

Some ways to free yourself from the bonds of materialism and worldly comfort:

- Donate excess items (Do you really need 18 pairs of shoes?).

- Give charitably — not just money, but also your talents and your time.

- Try a simple prayer like this one: "Jesus, help me detach from the things of this world, and focus on the glories of Your coming Kingdom!"

- Choose one "creature comfort" you could sacrifice for a day, a week, a Lenten season, etc. Many Catholics choose to give something up every Friday of the year in recognition of Jesus' death on Good Friday (meat is the classic one, but I personally give up sweets, and you could choose something else entirely).

Sin and Addictions

The Martins went to Confession regularly because they knew this Sacrament was a gift from God to keep them free from the bonds of sin. Though we may hate the idea of sin, we find that attachment to our particular "sin of choice" can be extremely powerful. The great St. Augustine once famously prayed, "Give me chastity and continence, but not yet."[56] (As a side note, you can see how beautifully Augustine's wayward story turned out in chapter 8 of this book, which is about his mother, St. Monica).

Today, millions of men and women struggle with attachment to internet pornography. Pornography takes something natural and good — sexual attraction, or *eros* in Greek — and disorders it by separating it from the self-giving love (*agape*) meant to accompany and fulfill it in sexual relationships.[57] Pornography objectifies human beings made in the likeness and image of God, and it poisons marriages. For some people, pornography can even become an addiction.

Whether it is to pornography, sex, gambling, a substance, or something else, addiction always hurts marriages. Addicts are utterly incapable of loving freely because they are slaves to their addictions. If you or your spouse is facing an addiction, you need to find help.

Some ways to free yourself from the bonds of sin and addiction:

- Go to Confession! Not only will you be freed from the chains of your past sins, but you will be empowered to keep those chains off in the future by the grace in that Sacrament.

- When you are tempted, pray, "God, through the grace of my last confession/last Eucharist, give me strength to overcome this temptation!"

- Avoid the "near occasion of sin:" situations that set you up for failure because they are fraught with temptation.

- If you struggle with attachment or addiction to internet pornography, you are far from alone. Seek the help of organizations such as Integrity Restored, Fortify, or Fight the New Drug which exist for this purpose.

- If you are battling a different addiction, such as alcoholism or drug use, you should also seek professional help breaking those chains (from Alcoholics Anonymous, Narcotics Anonymous, etc.). Get yourself the help you need.

Free to Love Forever

Saints Louis and Zélie Martin sought to free themselves of all attachments to sin, anxiety, and creature comforts so that they could freely choose love for one another and for God. We can all do the same! On your wedding day, you freely gave yourself to your spouse. Remain free and in control of your own will so that you can choose to love them anew today, tomorrow, and every day of your marriage.

PRAYER

Saints Louis and Zélie Martin,
after having had the desire for religious life,
you heard the Lord's call to the vocation of marriage.

You are the "parents without equal" of whom your daughter,
Saint Thérèse of the Child Jesus speaks;
the fortunate parents of Léonie, the Servant of God,
Sister Françoise-Thérèse;
of Marie, Pauline, and Céline, transplanted to Mount Carmel;
and of the four children
taken from your affection in their youth:
Hélène, Joseph, Jean-Baptiste, and Mélanie-Thérèse.

You gave all glory to God through your humble and patient
work, your commitment to the poor,
and your family life, where reigned the happiness
of loving and being loved.

You lived your daily life concretely through the joys
and sorrows of your existence.

You love us as your own children, with the heart
of a father and the heart of a mother,
because you are the friends of God.

Listen to our prayer … and intercede for us with
God the Father, through Jesus Christ our Lord,
in the grace of the Holy Spirit. Amen.

— From the shrine of Sts. Louis and Zélie
in Alençon, France[58]

QUESTIONS FOR DISCUSSION AND REFLECTION

1. What was something about the Martin family that surprised you? Is there any routine habit or practice from their lives that you want to try in your own family?

2. After reading this chapter, how would you define the vow to "love freely?" In what ways did Sts. Louis and Zélie live out this vow?

3. Saints Louis and Zélie chose to live simply and give freely to the needy. What material goods are you particularly attached to? How could your family live more simply?

4. The Martins were regular confessors. When was the last time you sought God's forgiveness and freedom from sin in the Sacrament of Reconciliation? What is holding you back from going to Confession again?

5. What does it mean to be "enslaved" by sin, anxiety, or worldliness? In what ways can a person free themselves from these chains?

CHAPTER 2

Loving Fully:
BLESSED BARBE ACARIE
(Bl. Marie of the Incarnation)

FEAST DAY: APRIL 18

The second vow of our marriage covenant is to love one another "totally," or "fully." This entails a mutual self-giving: each spouse gives their full gift of self and accepts the full gift of the other. We rejoice with our spouse in their successes and strengths, but also love their shortcomings and the crosses they carry. Moreover, we offer lifelong assistance in overcoming those shortcomings and carrying those crosses. For me, loving my husband *fully* means that I am his partner and "helpmate" for life.

Blessed Barbe Acarie, best known for founding the French Carmel, is a great example of partnership in marriage. Her husband, Pierre, was a good man, but not always prudent. Pierre's poor financial and political decisions landed him in a heap of trouble. Barbe could have abandoned him. She could have cut herself and her children loose of his problems. Instead, she rolled up her sleeves and worked to defend her husband's honor and keep her family together.

Pierre Acarie had some real shortcomings, but he was blessed to have a wife who would aid him in the fallout they caused and love him fully through the whole process. Let's meet this holy woman, observe how she lived out the vow to love fully, and find some ways that we can do the same.

Birth and Childhood

Barbara (Barbe) Avrillot was born on Feb. 1, 1566, in Paris, France, and baptized the next day. Her parents, Nicholas and Marie Avrillot, were both from the upper class of Parisian society; Nicholas was the accountant general in the Chamber of Paris and chancellor to Queen Margaret of Valois. The first few Avrillot children had died in infancy, so when Barbe was born healthy her mother wanted to offer some gift back in thanksgiving to God. Marie consecrated Barbe to the Blessed Virgin and to St. Claude, dressing her in white for the first seven years of her life.[1] It would prove a fitting start for this pure and holy woman.

Barbe was educated by Franciscan nuns at Longchamp, and she felt drawn to their lifestyle from an early age. She was chosen as an intern for the Order of St. Clare at age 11 and allowed to receive her First Holy Communion at 12 (three or four years earlier than usual at the time). Barbe was noticeably pious for her age, frequently attending Mass and Confession.

Young Adulthood and Marriage

As Barbe grew older, it became clear that her mother wanted her to marry and not stay with her beloved Poor Clares. Barbe was willing to go to any other convent of Marie's choice, but Marie insisted she find a husband instead. Barbe tried to accept her mother's plans for her life, but in her sadness, she spent a lot of time in her room. Her mother punished her harshly for avoiding social engagements — even to an abusive level. For example, Barbe was not allowed to have a fire in her room in the winter, and eventually she had to have several toe joints amputated due to chilblains, painful swelling of tiny blood vessels due to the cold.[2]

In 1584, when Barbe was 16, Marie Avrillot arranged her marriage to Pierre Acarie, the viscount of Villemor. Pierre was a religious man who had previously considered a vocation to the priesthood. He prayed the Divine Office daily, enjoyed spiritual reading, and spent his free time helping local priests. Pierre was also very involved with the Catholic League of France, which would cause major ramifications for his family. While marriage may not have been Barbe's first choice, she was set on loving God "with her whole heart" in this vocation. She aspired to fulfill "her marital duties with the highest possible degree of perfection."[3]

Barbe had always dressed in plain clothes out of humility, despite her family's wealth. Pierre was more concerned with appearances, and he expected his wife to dress like a noblewoman. Though it was difficult for her, Barbe was obedient to Pierre just as she had been obedient to her mother and the Poor Clares. Dressed in her finery, Barbe soon found herself starting to care more about image. Comparing her appearance to other women often brought her down, and she hated these moments where she lost her usual peace. Barbe realized that if her mind were always truly fixed on God, and not on appearances, she would never lose that peace for even a moment.[4]

Early in their marriage, Barbe took to reading romance novels. Worried that this kind of reading material would not direct Barbe's heart towards God, Pierre asked a priest friend to procure some spiritual reading for his wife. From then on Barbe used her free time to learn more about the saints and her Catholic faith.[5] God was definitely working through Pierre to shape Barbe's future, because reading about one saint, St. Teresa of Ávila, would one day change her life. Pierre was loving his wife fully by helping her find a way to grow in virtue through her hobby of reading.

Motherhood and Home Life

Together, the Acaries had six children between 1584 and 1592: Nicolas, Marie, Pierre, Jehan, Marguerite, and Geneviève. Barbe "made religion beautiful and delightful" to her children.[6] They prayed the Mass and the Divine Office together every day. She taught her children to genuinely love their neighbor as themselves, and to treat even the handful of servants they employed as respected members of the family.

Barbe was extremely careful about the company her children kept. If her family was invited to a wedding with other morally questionable guests, Barbe would briefly leave Paris so she had an excuse to politely decline. She had her children confess every wrongdoing to her, and if she ever caught them in a lie, she was strict with them. This was all in love, however, and the Acarie children grew quickly in virtue. One of her daughters asserted that, even after 20 years in a convent, she "never learned anything more perfect ... than she had practiced" at home with Barbe.[7]

Barbe had high expectations of her servants' faith lives as well. Barbe's personal maid, Andrée Levois, became a dear friend, and was treated as an equal in seeking virtue and growing in faith. All the servants of the household were expected to join the Acaries at Sunday Mass at the local parish, St. Gervais. They were also required to attend Madame Acarie's daily discussions on virtue and spiritual growth. Barbe's children, servants, and friends often sought out one-on-one spiritual direction with her. Not only was she wise and gentle, but Barbe was purported to have many gifts that made her a wonderful spiritual guide, including prophecy, reading hearts, and discerning spirits.[8]

Habits of Faith

Impressively, Barbe grew in her own spirituality even while raising six kids and running a household. She was deeply affected by these words from St. Augustine: "He is a miser indeed, to whom God is not enough."[9] Soon after reading and meditating on this quote, around 1590, Barbe started having mystical experiences. For example, she would sometimes fall into ecstasies during prayer or Mass because she was so drawn into the holiness of the Blessed Sacrament. At first, these experiences worried Barbe, but she slowly learned to control her mysticism more and to appreciate this gift from God. Barbe was encouraged in her faith by her circle of holy friends, including St. Francis de Sales and St. Vincent de Paul. [10]

Barbe knew that virtue must be honed constantly, so she practiced many personal sacrifices. She usually had only one meal a day and did not sleep much because she was up late praying and awake early for daily Mass. Her spiritual directors were wary of these practices, and sometimes tried to talk her out of them. Barbe simply explained that her sacrifices had been revealed to her by the Holy Spirit. Who could argue with that? Furthermore, her health never seemed to be harmed by these mortifications; to the contrary, she seemed healthier than ever. Barbe Acarie also suffered another beautiful pain: she was the first French woman gifted with the (invisible but attested) stigmata, open wounds that mirror the nail marks in the hands, feet, and side of Christ.

Ministry and Aid for the Needy

Madame Acarie was known to take prostitutes in to stay at the "Hôtel Acarie," as the family home was often called. She helped them find another way to make ends meet. She also established the Community of St. Geneviève, inviting around 20 women preparing themselves for Carmelite life to live in her home. Unfortunately, Pierre Acarie's loud and silly behavior often distracted these women from their work and prayer. Barbe solved this problem by relocating the Community, but she did not speak ill of her husband in the process. [11] She continued to love Pierre fully — not despite, but with, his boisterous personality.

Barbe also took up many ministries outside her home. She worked to stir up renewed zeal in lukewarm religious communities, made vestments for missionaries, and sewed silk gowns for the poor so that they would not be ridiculed for their poverty. Barbe's local community appointed her to direct food donations during a famine. Most of all, Barbe loved visiting the sick at local hospitals like the Hôtel Dieu, alongside the nuns she had adored as a child. M. Gauthier, a future partner in her quest to bring the Carmelites to France, claimed that Barbe saved "at least ten thousand souls" in her community.[12] After reading about her life, that figure sounds believable.

Few details survive about Pierre's involvement in Barbe's ministries, inside or outside of their home. He seemed to be more interested in politics and spent most of his time with his friends from the Catholic League. However, Pierre must have been at least somewhat supportive of Barbe's work because it affected his own life. There were nuns-to-be down the hall and ex-prostitutes sitting at the dinner table, and he never sent them away.

Harder Times

Everything was going smoothly in the Hôtel Acarie through these early years of marriage and parenthood, but Barbe could see a dark cloud approaching for her family. She was aware that all the members of the Catholic League were in a precarious spot politically, and that Pierre would be particularly at-risk as a leader of the group. Additionally, she had concerns about her husband's financial prudence. However, Barbe was a humble and obedient wife, and she trusted God with her family's future despite her misgivings.

The trouble Barbe predicted arrived with the eighth (and final) French War of Religion, which started in 1584. King Henry III was Catholic, but had named a Calvinist heir, also named Henry. French Catholics opposed to a Protestant king endorsed a different candidate named — you guessed it — Henry. Pierre Acarie was one of 16 men leading this resistance movement within the Catholic League.[13]

A complicated chain of events ensued, made even more difficult to follow because all the major players have the same first name. In the end, Calvinist Henry (more commonly known as Henry of Navarre, or King Henry IV) took the throne in 1589. After landing on the losing side of the battle, Pierre was lucky that Henry IV didn't have him killed. Instead, Pierre was simply exiled from Paris in 1593. Pierre chose to spend his exile living like a monk in a cell at the Carthusian monastery of Bourgfontaine.

Barbe's Response

Meanwhile, 28-year-old Barbe was left behind with six young children and a messy financial situation. Pierre had been much more generous than prudent with his wealth, lending substantial sums of money to other members of the League. Now that the group was largely disbanded and he himself was exiled, Pierre had no money left to pay his own debts. Barbe began selling off furniture and family heirlooms, and even had to beg in the streets for money at times to feed her children. One evening, debt collectors actually broke into the Acaries' home during dinner and took away the chairs and plates being used by the family! Still, when family members begged Barbe to at least save her own dowry and separate her fortune from her husband's, she refused: "[T]o this Madame Acarie would never consent. She said that no human consideration should induce her to make any division of goods when God had bound them together, and added that she loved her husband too much not to share all his misfortunes."[14]

Barbe and Pierre were bound together by God on their wedding day, and they were bound together still beneath this heavy cross of exile and debt. To love Pierre fully, Barbe had to love his burden, too. She would not leave him to carry it alone.

So, Barbe set to work aiding her husband. First, she sent her children off to school or to relatives. Being separated from her children was painful for such a tender and devoted mother, but she needed to devote her full attention to the complicated situation at hand. Barbe spent nearly all her time waiting in endless lines at courts, writing letters to people who might be helpful, and visiting her husband. Being a woman certainly didn't expedite the process for her; neither did being the wife of a man accused of treason. Nevertheless, Barbe pushed forward in her quest to have Pierre acquitted of his alleged crimes.

Barbe had other problems to deal with as well. During one of her trips to visit Pierre, she was thrown from a horse and gravely injured. She was at least partially lame for the rest of her life, and often experienced intense pain when she walked, but Barbe kept her suffering hidden as much as possible.

With Barbe's hard work, the situation gradually improved. Pierre was cleared of several false charges, and it looked like he might soon be allowed to return to Paris. Then, Pierre suddenly disappeared from the monastery. Another opposed division of the Catholic League had taken him prisoner! Barbe was somehow able to scrape together the ransom money, and in 1596 the family was finally reunited in the Hôtel Acarie after three years of separation.[15]

Founding the French Carmel

During the family's legal struggles, Barbe lived with her younger cousin, future cardinal M. Bérulle, for a time. He and Barbe helped each other deepen their spirituality throughout this time. M. Bérulle eventually became Barbe's main partner in bringing the Discalced Carmelite order of nuns to France, the work for which she is most famous.

That story began with the spiritual reading Pierre had suggested to his wife. After reading a biography of St. Teresa of Ávila, Barbe became captivated with this woman and the charism of the order of nuns she founded. Discalced Carmelites live a life centered around prayer: they spend at least two hours a day in silent prayer in addition to praying the Liturgy of the Hours. For Carmelites, prayer is not a secretive thing between an individual and God, but an important topic of discussion in spiritual direction, and a skill that can be honed.[16] All of this resonated deeply with Barbe Acarie, as she always prioritized her own prayer life, had tremendous respect for her spiritual directors, and did a fair amount of spiritual direction herself. In 1601, soon after Barbe had finished reading the foundress' biography, St. Teresa of Ávila actually appeared to her. Saint Teresa told Barbe that God was calling her to bring the Discalced Carmelite order to France.

At first, Barbe was convinced by her friend and spiritual advisor, St. Francis de Sales, to wait and see if the visions returned to be sure they were real. Ever obedient, Barbe waited. Eight months later, when St. Teresa appeared to Barbe again, St. Francis himself helped her get papal permission to bring current Teresian nuns to France from Spain. Barbe insisted that nuns from Ávila come personally to set up the French convents, because only they could ensure that every detail would be exactly as it was in Spain. By 1603, just two years after Barbe's initial visions of St. Teresa, the Discalced Carmelites were established in France.

Barbe was instrumental in the founding of at least four Carmelite convents, or Carmels, and all three of her daughters eventually became Carmelite nuns.[17] Her middle daughter, Marguerite, entered before she was even 16. Geneviéve, the youngest, followed, and last was Marie, Barbe's eldest daughter. Marie struggled for years with the decision between the convent and marriage, afraid to be ruled by either. Madame Acarie took her daughter on a pilgrimage to Notre Dame de Liesse, and this finally cleared things up for Marie.

Barbe was careful with her daughters' vocations, just as she had been for the young women she had sponsored throughout her life. She did not force or even encourage religious life for fear it may not be their true calling. Madame Acarie wrote that, even if she had a hundred children and was unable to care for them, she would not send one of them into a convent unless she was absolutely sure it was their vocation because she feared "upsetting God's plans."[18] To this end, Barbe also helped establish the Ursuline order in France to give women without a Carmelite disposition another option. She had great respect for the Ursulines, who served as teachers, because they passed on Catholic values and virtues to the next generation.

Pierre's Death and Barbe's Widowed Years

In 1613, after 31 years of marriage, Pierre fell ill. The illness did not seem serious to the doctors or to Pierre himself, but God revealed to Barbe that her husband was dying. When she told him, Pierre believed her and quickly received the Last Rites. People in attendance noted that he took this Sacrament very seriously. Just before he died, Pierre also begged Barbe to forgive him for everything he had made her suffer throughout their marriage. He thanked her for everything she had done for him, for loving his faults and strengths alike, and for all the crosses she had carried with him as his wife.

Barbe Acarie saw her childhood dream fulfilled when she entered the convent as a 49-year-old widow in 1615. She humbly asked to be admitted as only a lay sister at the poorest Carmel. This led her to Amiens, where her daughter Marguerite was sub-prioress. Barbe took the name Sister Marie of the Incarnation. Sister Marie was quiet, usually found in the kitchen peeling potatoes. She exuded joy in every small task that she was given, giving herself as fully to this vocation as to her previous vocation to marriage.[19] Sister Marie also showed a "special and tender devotion for her sisters who were sick and suffering,"[20] caring for them just as she had for her husband, children, and even household servants when they had been ill.

By this time, though, Sister Marie was in poor health herself. After a long struggle with illness, she died in 1618, during Holy Week. She was 52 years old.

Beatification and Example to the Faithful

Sister Marie of the Incarnation was beatified by Pope Pius VI in 1791. She may be better known by her Carmelite name, but most of the saintly work of this woman's life was actually accomplished during her married years, while she was simply Barbe Acarie.

Barbe and her husband Pierre were married for 31 years and raised six children together. All three of their daughters became Carmelite nuns, one of whom is now on her own path to sainthood as Ven. Margaret of the Blessed Sacrament. One of their sons also became a priest. This speaks volumes about the community of faith the Acaries created in their home.

Even though their house was already bustling with family, Barbe and Pierre welcomed countless others into the Hôtel Acarie, from ex-prostitutes to future nuns. The Acaries were also involved in other ministries to aid local priests, the poor, and the sick. The entire community looked to Barbe as a source of wisdom and spiritual guidance. Pierre may not have always acted wisely, but he was blessed with a wife who loved him with all his faults and crosses.

Marital Vow: Loving Fully

When Pierre Acarie was exiled and powerless, all his burdens and entanglements fell to his wife's responsibility. Barbe endured the ensuing financial hardship, separation from her family, and vicious rumors about her husband with grace and perseverance. She had accepted her husband's full gift of self — flaws, debts, and all — and in these hard times she had to step up and give of herself fully in turn.

Catholics striving to live out the vow to love our spouses fully can imitate the mutual self-giving and support we see in Barbe's marriage. We must also combat any modern practices that threaten our ability to make a total gift of self. Finally, we can learn how to guard against the concept of being "incomplete" without a spouse and maintain our identities as unique individuals within a healthy marriage partnership.

Giving and Receiving the Full Gift of Self

What does it look like to struggle with loving fully? A wife struggling with *giving* her whole self might avoid introducing her husband to her friends or consciously hide some details from her past. It can be scary to give your whole self to someone, even your spouse, because you face rejection. More specific thoughts like *What if he finds my friends boring?* and *What will he think of me if he finds out about my past?* are really pointing towards one deeper question: *If I was fully known, would I still be fully loved?* When we stop to think about it, though, it isn't even possible to be fully loved if you are not fully known.

Struggling with *receiving* your spouse's full gift of self is the opposite problem. Pierre Acarie, for example, did not accept Barbe's desire to dress more simply. This might also look like a wife who gets easily irritated with her husband's shyness. These spouses probably wonder *Why does she insist on looking so plain?* or *Why can't he just fake it and be more friendly?* The deeper level to these questions is often, *Why can't my spouse be more like me?* Frustrating as spousal differences can be, at the end of the day I am thankful to have a husband who balances me out and helps me see things from another perspective.

Saint Paul tells us that "God proves his love for us in that *while we were still sinners* Christ died for us" (Rom 5:8; emphasis mine). Even at our worst, God loved us fully, and gave us the complete gift of Himself. In return, He wants all of you — your whole heart, mind, and soul. Your spouse deserves to fully love and be loved by you, too.

A few ways to more fully give and receive the gift of self:

- Think about your past. If there is any topic you have avoided talking to your spouse about, start that conversation.

- Talk with your spouse about each of your weaknesses, quirks, and struggles. Note ways that you balance one another out and make a stronger team.

- Especially on rough days when you are bickering, ask your spouse, "How can I make your life easier today?" Be his or her helpmate in carrying the daily load.

- Try a simple prayer like this one: "Lord, by the grace of my marriage, empower me to help carry my spouse's burden."

Modern Challenges to Loving Fully

Barbe was urged to separate herself financially from her husband when things went wrong. Today, couples often go into their marriage prepared to do the same by creating prenuptial agreements. Even more common is premarital cohabitation, which allows a couple to "test drive" marriage without actually committing to one another.

And then there is contraception, seemingly accepted by everyone in society. The Church, however, warns that contraception not only bars a couple from fulfilling their vow to love fruitfully (more on that in chapter 4!), but also to love fully. When a couple uses contraception, the husband tells his wife, "I accept all parts of you ... except your natural, functioning fertility. We need to repress that part of you." A woman on the Pill does not give her whole self to her husband in their sexual intimacy, but instead holds back from him an amazing gift: the ability to share with her and with God in the miracle that is the creation of new life.

No matter how popular prenups, cohabitation, and contraception become, these practices hold a couple back from a total gift of self. Karol Wojtyła, the future Pope St. John Paul II, warned strictly against their adoption. Instead, married people should strive for "the *fullness* of self-surrender" and "the *completeness* of personal commitment."[21]

Are you giving your full gift of self to your spouse? If not, what are you holding back, and why?

A few ways to combat these modern challenges:

- If you are not yet married and have considered/chosen one of these practices, talk with the priest preparing you for marriage about how these choices can harm your marriage.

- Educate yourself about using Natural Family Planning (NFP) in place of contraception, discussed more in chapter 4: Loving Fruitfully.

- Talk with a couple who has been married for many years about how their choices to avoid prenuptial agreements, cohabitation, and contraception have affected their marriage.

Enriching One Another

To love your spouse completely, you yourself must already be complete. Spouses' strengths and weaknesses often balance with one another, and it is wonderful when spouses help one another to grow and mature. However, a person who lacks confidence, capability, or personal identity should not get married hoping their spouse will "fill in the gaps" and solve all their problems. This is not what marriage does. Instead of seeking to complete or be completed by his wife, a spiritually mature husband sees in his wife another already-complete human person whom he is "content to be able to *enrich* ... with the gift of himself."[22]

Loving fully does not mean that husband and wife meld together into one identity, either.[23] Barbe and Pierre each had their own interests, such as the Catholic League or preparing women for the convent. Likewise, though we have become "one flesh" in the Sacrament of Holy Matrimony, my husband and I still have unique interests, goals, and relationships. I write and play the piano; Chris does leatherwork and paints. I enjoy going out with a group of friends; Chris prefers quiet evenings at home. We each have our own "things," but we encourage one another along the way. Like Pierre guiding his wife's reading, Chris and I also try to help each other stay on a path to holiness through our unique activities.

A few ways to improve in these areas:

- If the two of you seem to do everything together, look for a small way to be your own unique people. Start with one evening a month that you each go out with separate friends or pursue a hobby that is not as interesting to your spouse.

- Ask your spouse for one concrete action you could do to support or encourage their hobbies or dreams.

- Talk with your spouse about how your interests and hobbies make you feel fulfilled. Brainstorm ways these interests and hobbies could better point you towards God.

Fullness of Self-Surrender

Marriage isn't 50/50 — it's 100/100. If we want to live out our marriage vow to love our spouse fully, we can't hold back any part of ourselves or reject any part of them. Blessed Barbe Acarie shows each of us how to be a true life partner to our spouse, sharing our joys and our burdens.

The following prayer by one of Barbe's spiritual friends and advisors, St. Francis de Sales, can be helpful for moments when those burdens feel too heavy. Pray that God will give you and your spouse superabundant grace from your sacramental marriage to carry (and even love!) your crosses straight to Heaven.

PRAYER

O my God, I thank you and I praise you for accomplishing
your holy and all-lovable will without any regard for mine.
With my whole heart, in spite of my heart,
do I receive this cross I feared so much!
It is the cross of Your choice, the cross of Your love.
I venerate it; nor for anything in the world
would I wish that it had not come,
since You willed it. I keep it with gratitude and with joy,
as I do everything that comes from Your hand;
and I shall strive to carry it without letting it drag,
with all the respect and all the affection
which Your works deserve. Amen.

— *"Act of Abandonment" of St. Francis de Sales,*
spiritual advisor to Bl. Barbe Acarie[24]

QUESTIONS FOR DISCUSSION AND REFLECTION

1. How does Bl. Barbe Acarie remind you of yourself? In what
   ways does she seem very different from you?

2. After reading this chapter, how would you define the vow
   to "love fully"? How did Bl. Barbe Acarie live out this particular vow?

3. Which of your hobbies and interests overlap with your
   spouse, and which do the two of you hold separately? Are
   you happy with the balance of individual and joint pursuits
   in your marriage?

4. What is one bullet point action item from this chapter that
   you want to try out? Why did you choose that one?

5. Think of one way your spouse is very different from you
   (e.g., introversion vs. extroversion; making detailed plans vs.
   "winging it;" talking things out vs. needing time alone to
   process). In what ways is this difference frustrating to you?
   In what ways might it help bring balance to your marriage?

CHAPTER 3

Loving Faithfully:
SAINT THOMAS MORE

FEAST DAY: JUNE 22

What does it mean to be faithful? Today, someone who occasionally attends church might be called a "faithful" Christian, and a "faithful" spouse is just one who doesn't cheat. These qualifications set the bar incredibly low for our most important relationships! A deeper understanding of faithful love can add depth to both our Christian faith and our marriages. True Christian faithfulness is remaining steadfastly committed to the covenant God made with us, His people. In the same way, true marital faithfulness is remaining steadfastly committed to the vows of the covenant we made with our spouses. The Englishman St. Thomas More is a great example to us of both.

Many biographers believe that Thomas More was named after St. Thomas á Becket, a man with whom he would share much more than just a name. The two men were born maybe 20 yards apart in the same London district; they both served as Chancellor of England under a King Henry (II and VIII, respectively); and ultimately, they were both executed for choosing the Church over their king. Despite his unjust imprisonment and martyrdom, St. Thomas More's story shows the true peace that comes from loving God and family faithfully to the very end.

Birth and Childhood

Thomas More was born in London, England, on Feb. 7, 1478. His father, John More, was a respected lawyer and judge, and the More family was "noted for its honour,"[1] though they were not of noble class. Thomas' mother, Agnes, was John More's first wife. She and three of Thomas' five siblings all died while Thomas was young, some possibly from a bad bout of plague in 1485. John had four wives in total, remarrying each time he was widowed. Thomas and his surviving siblings had only one consistent maternal figure: a caretaker called "Mother Mawd," who was a devout Christian. Mawd's faith absolutely rubbed off on young Thomas.

Thomas attended one of the best grammar schools in London, where his studies likely focused on the Latin language and literature. In his day, many people conversed in Latin as much as they did in English, and almost all of Thomas More's letters are written in Latin. Young Thomas loved reading and music, but according to several friends, he was not a great singer. Later in life, he found an instrument that suited him — and his listeners — better: the lute.

At 12, Thomas was chosen as a page for John Morton, the archbishop of Canterbury and Chancellor of England. At 14, Morton nominated Thomas as a "scholarship boy," and Thomas headed off to study at Canterbury College within Oxford University at 14, which was the average age to begin college at that time.

Higher Education

At Oxford, Thomas learned about the Bible, Canon Law, and the writings of Aristotle. He also wrote accomplished poetry and became interested in the humanist movement, which emphasized the value of all human beings. He enjoyed the quasi-monastic schedule at Oxford. Like many saints, Thomas was very drawn to parts of monasticism. During his early years practicing law (1499-1503), he lived in the guesthouse of the Charterhouse Monastery in London. Though Thomas eventually married, he never lost the devotion to silent prayer he learned from the Carthusians at the monastery.

At his father's urging, Thomas left Oxford without completing a degree to pursue law at the Inns of Chancery, professional organizations for English barristers. He began at the New Inn at 16, and by 18 he advanced to Lincoln's Inn, where his father was a senior member. Thomas' studies reinforced his central worldview that there was "no essential...difference between law and Church."[2] He would have to defend this opinion throughout his life against Reformation-era thinkers overemphasizing the idea that the law is "written on our hearts" to debase the tradition and precedent of the Church.

Studying for the bar was a long road, but Thomas More was finally named a full member of the law profession in 1501 or 1502. He had all the qualities of a fine lawyer — he was "precise and shrewd," "cautious ... theatrical, persuasive and practical."[3] More valued justice deeply not only as a lawyer, but as a faithful Catholic and a concerned humanist. "Were it my father stood on the one side and the devil on the other," he once wrote, "his cause being good, the devil should have right."[4]

Married Life

After he had discerned out of monastic life and established himself as a lawyer, Thomas felt ready to marry. Jane Colt, the daughter of a friend, was only 17 when the couple married in 1505, while Thomas was ten years her senior. Together, they had four children: Margaret (Meg), Elizabeth, Cecily, and John. Their marriage seems to have been happy. Thomas tutored his wife in music and literature and described her as *facillima* — most good-natured.[5] The More family had a library of at least thirty books — very impressive for that time — and a private chapel for their daily habits of prayer. Sadly, Jane died after just six years of marriage, likely while giving birth to a fifth, stillborn child.

Thomas grieved the loss of his first wife but had good reason to remarry in a hurry: his four young children needed a mother. Soon after Jane's death, Thomas married 41-year-old Alice Harper Middleton, a widow and old friend. Alice and Thomas More did not have any biological children together, but Alice brought one daughter (also named Alice) from her previous marriage, and the Mores eventually took in two wards in the coming years: Margaret and Anne. Thomas and his son John were certainly outnumbered in a household full of women!

Alice More was not quite so beautiful or as *facillima* as Jane had been. She is described as "plain-speaking," "forceful," and even "imperious," and Thomas More himself wrote to his wife, "I never found you willing to be ruled yet."[6] But Alice was also a fastidious housekeeper and a committed mother to her child and stepchildren. Thomas felt he could "rely completely" on his worthy wife.[7] She made him laugh with her witty comments, and she never shied away from entering religious discussions with him. Thomas' close friend, the Dutch humanist Desiderius Erasmus, intimated that Thomas was actually somewhat in awe of his wife, and always approached her with "playful flattery" rather than "authority and severity."[8]

Fatherhood

Thomas was very devoted to his children, who in turn confided everything to him. He formed special, unique bonds with each child, but Thomas was especially attached to his eldest daughter Margaret, called Meg. As a young adult, Meg was tasked with washing the itchy hairshirt her father wore under his clothing since his days in the monastery, because she was the only person he trusted to tell about this act of penance. Even Alice did not know the shirt existed. Once, when Meg fell terribly ill, her father pleaded with God to spare her life. Thomas vowed that if Meg died of her illness, he would resign from all his positions because he would be too depressed to carry on.[9] Fortunately, Meg recovered, and lived with or near her beloved father for the rest of his life.

As he became busier in his advancing career, Thomas wrote almost daily to his children, and encouraged them to write back to him. He was "greatly pleased" by their "charming" and refreshing letters, and he considered letter writing an important part of their education.[10] Thomas More deeply valued education, not only for his son but equally for his daughters, which was a countercultural idea at the time. Even Thomas' *"derlynge"* (darling) friend Erasmus did not see the value in educating women until he conversed with the More girls.[11] Meg in particular was known to be one of the most educated women in England and became the first non-royal English woman ever to publish a book she had translated into English.[12]

Mea schola, as Thomas called the school forming within his home, was run by carefully selected tutors, who were frequently assisted or overseen by Alice More. The domestic school grew, and eventually as many as 13 children, wards, and grandchildren may have attended at once! The tutors focused on Greek, Latin, astronomy, philosophy, logic, and music, but all of these were intertwined with religious studies. Erasmus described the home as "a school and gymnasium of the Christian religion."[13] The rhythms of daily prayer and biblical reading in the More household echoed the customs Thomas had come to love in the monastery. He found joy in the peace and order of his Domestic Church-School.

Advancing Career

Meanwhile, Thomas' career was advancing quickly. He served as a burgess, under-sheriff of London, Chancellor of the Duchy of Lancaster, and High Steward at both Oxford and Cambridge. His reputation for quick and fair decisions earned him a senior reader position within Lincoln's Inn by 1515. In autumn 1516, Thomas was appointed to the king's Star Chamber council, alongside his father, John More. Thomas knew that being a councilor of the king was both a powerful and a dangerous position. What if his faith and the king's will did not align?

Initially, King Henry VIII and Thomas had a very stable relationship. By 1519, Thomas was the king's second secretary, mainly drafting letters dictated by the king to Cardinal Thomas Wolsey, the Lord Chancellor of England. Thomas knew all the intimate details about deals with foreign courts; he held the ciphers to secret messages; he was "entirely trusted by both men."[14] In 1521, Sir Thomas More was knighted as under-treasurer, and two years later king and chancellor chose him to be Speaker of Parliament.

In all these appointments, Thomas "did not seek, he acquiesced."[15] Not only was he humble, but, more pressingly, Thomas yearned for a simpler life that allowed him more time at home with his family. Even when he was away for short periods of time, Thomas "longed" to see his children again and to "rest in the bosom" of his wife.[16] Sometimes, he even held back his wit and insight so that he would not be invited to as many royal dinners.

Alas, Thomas' brilliance, mirth, and faithfulness continued to earn him increasingly lofty — and dangerous — positions.

The King's "Great Matter"

It was no secret that King Henry VIII was dissatisfied with his wife, Catherine of Aragon. Henry wanted a male heir, but Catherine had borne only a daughter and several stillborn sons. Henry believed he should be granted an annulment, but Thomas and many other Catholics quietly disagreed. Thomas hoped this issue, which came to be known as the King's "Great Matter," would never boil over. He walked a thin line, listening carefully to all the counselors sent to change his mind about the annulment, but, in the end, holding fast to his defense of the indissolubility of marriage. He knew that what God had joined, in his own or King Henry's marriage, no man could break.

In 1529, Lord Chancellor Wolsey was sent to Rome to obtain the papal annulment. When he returned empty handed, he was arrested for treason, and Henry, wishing to "teach the Church, both in Rome and England, a lesson in power,"[17] appointed in Wolsey's place the first lay Chancellor in almost 100 years: Sir Thomas More.

Sir Thomas More served as Lord Chancellor of England for 31 months. He was tasked with combating heresy and defending the Church, something he had already been doing through his writing. In his most famous work, *Utopia* ("no place"), Thomas warned of the results of godless government. *Utopia*, published in 1516, has since been used to examine the failures of communism. Thomas wrote long letters to Protestants like Martin Luther and William Tyndale, boldly supporting the unity of the Catholic Church, and specific traditions they had attacked. As Lord Chancellor, Thomas published lists of prohibited heretical books and counselled imprisoned heretics to guide them towards proper understanding and appreciation of the faith. This role suited him perfectly in some ways. In it, his duty to country and Church came together; his knowledge of the law and of the traditions of Catholicism were both put to good use.

By early 1532, a frustrated King Henry had begun to trust other advisers, especially Thomas Cromwell, over Thomas More. Cromwell helped Henry establish primacy in England over the Pope in Rome. Cromwell's efforts often infringed directly on More's responsibilities as Lord Chancellor. In Cromwell's "Submission of the Clergy," all legislative powers formerly allowed to the Church were given instead to Parliament, and royal assent was required for any change to Canon Law to be recognized in England. Here was true, terrifying heresy: the king, and not the Pope, would be head of the English Church.

Jesus Himself had founded the papacy, establishing St. Peter as the first head of His earthly Church. Therefore, Thomas declared that he could not sign anything that gave the king primacy over the current Pope "without the jeopardizing of [his] soul to perpetual damnation."[18] Thomas had always been faithful to the king, but he knew he had to be faithful to his Church first. The day after the edict was published, May 16, 1532, Sir Thomas More resigned as Chancellor.

Back at Home

After his resignation, Thomas returned home with his future uncertain. He probably knew that he was headed for imprisonment or even execution. The situation only worsened when Thomas, who was still a counselor to the king, did not attend the coronation of Henry's new queen, Anne Boleyn. Still, Thomas tried to focus on his family and faith in the time he had remaining. He continued his daily prayer, and often devoted the entirety of each Friday in his private chapel, meditating on the Passion of Christ. Thomas took up deeper penances during this time, too. He fasted frequently, and when he ate, his meals were simple. He went to bed by nine each night, so that he could wake as early as two o'clock in the morning to work and pray before daily Mass.[19]

Thomas enjoyed having more time with his growing family during these months. By this point, the household included several of his children's spouses, including William Roper, who was husband to the beloved Meg and Thomas' first biographer. There were also several grandchildren, servants, tutors for *Mea Schola,* and even a jester or "fool." More saw true value in humor. He was a very witty and joyful man himself, and he reveled in being called "foolish" by men like Martin Luther, because foolishness defends against pridefulness. Another aspect of the household that invited joy and silliness was Alice's "menagerie" of animals including a fox, a weasel, and even a small monkey!

Thomas also used this time to recommit to his acts of charity. He was known to stay up all night praying for local women who were in labor, which is especially poignant if his first wife and fifth child did indeed die during labor. Thomas visited the home he had set up years before for the poor, sick, and elderly. Meg had overseen this home while he had been busy with his duties for work. Soon she would have to take it over completely.

Thomas Imprisoned

In April 1534, Sir Thomas More was officially called forward to sign his name to the oath of supremacy of the English Crown over the Pope. At his refusal, he was accused of high treason and sent to the Tower of London to await trial.

The conditions of Thomas' 15 months of imprisonment were not horrible. He had a small brick stove, a pallet bed, and a table and chair for his reading and writing. He was often allowed to walk around the property, and he was even attended by a trusted servant. Most importantly to Thomas, he was able to participate in the Sacrifice of the Mass each day. He also had more time than ever before for prayer, spiritual reading, and writing; as Peter Ackroyd puts it, "He had become a monk at last."[20]

Thomas knew it was vitally important to steel himself in his faith through this extra prayer and silence so that he would not give in to signing the oath. Furthermore, if he were to die for his "treason," he needed to prepare his soul for eternity. In the Tower, Thomas especially meditated on the Passion of Christ, the subject of one of his treatises. He yearned to imitate Christ in facing those men who wanted him to recant and betray his conscience; at the same time, he did not want to incite too much anger because he didn't feel worthy of martyrdom. For this reason, Thomas' main strategy was silence. If he stayed silent about why he would not sign the oath, there would be no proof that his reasons were treasonous, and he could not be justly sentenced to execution.

Nevertheless, Thomas was not afraid of death, and was determined to remain stalwart. His beloved family never truly understood. As we see in the 1966 Oscar-winning movie "A Man for All Seasons" (based on Robert Bolt's acclaimed play), Meg and Alice both claimed that God would know what was truly in Thomas' heart even if he signed the oath to save his life. These statements did not change Thomas' mind, but they did make the decision more painful. Thomas wrote that, if his family was more encouraging, he might "merrily run to death."[21] He also worried about the safety and financial stability of his family without him. He had moved valuable goods away from his estate for safekeeping before he was jailed, in hopes that they would eventually be of use to Alice, his children, and his grandchildren.

Trial and Death

The jury at Thomas' trial in the early summer of 1535 included three members of the family of Anne Boleyn, Henry's new queen. The evidence against him was obviously baseless. Thomas defended himself nobly, but it was in vain — he was convicted of high treason and sentenced to a gruesome death within 15 minutes. After the trial, William Roper recorded that Meg, "seized and overcome with great grief and sorrow ... rushed up to her father and threw her arms about his neck, holding him tightly ... without being able to say a word."[22] No words would have been adequate. The world was losing one of its greatest thinkers, Christendom one of its greatest defenders, and the More family a dear, faithful husband and father.

Nevertheless, Thomas More, who frequently described himself as "merry," managed to make even the last minutes of his life mirthful. He asked for help climbing the stairs to his beheading but joked that, afterwards, he could make it back down fine on his own. He forgave his prosecutors and executioner, sincerely hoping that he and they "may yet hereafter in Heaven merrily all meet together" like St. Stephen, the first Christian martyr, and St. Paul, who participated in Stephen's stoning. Just before he died, Sir Thomas More famously professed himself "the King's good servant, but God's first" — faithful to both, but in due order.[23]

Thomas' Canonization

The conditions of Thomas' death did not faze him, because what mattered was that he was bound for eternal glory with God. More himself put it best: "Now to this great glory can no man come headless. Our head is Christ."[24]

Thomas More was canonized by Pope Pius XI in 1935, exactly 400 years after his martyrdom. For a famously martyred intellectual giant, he is a surprisingly relatable saint to many people. Thomas has become the patron saint of people from his career fields — lawyers, civil servants, and politicians.

Saint Thomas More is also the patron saint of adopted children because he took in several wards and welcomed his children's spouses as his own children, too. Meg's husband,

William Roper, for example, was converted back to Catholicism from Lutheranism by his father-in-law's prayers. After Thomas' death, William helped Meg run the poorhouse Thomas had founded, and William himself was later incarcerated in the Tower for aiding Catholic refugees. William was not the only one who took inspiration from Thomas More: He was a hero to thousands of faithful English Catholics facing intolerance, exclusion, and even hatred as the Anglican Church took root in the years after his death.

Marital Vow: Loving Faithfully

Sometimes committing yourself exclusively to one person for life can seem daunting. The media certainly doesn't glorify this kind of faithfulness: promiscuity and affairs are not only shrugged off but sometimes even celebrated in movies and TV shows. But our hearts were made for so much more. As Bobby and Jackie Angel put it, "We all ache for faithful love because we were made in the image of God, who is faithful."[25]

Whenever I look up and see a rainbow, I am reminded of God's faithfulness to His promise never to flood the earth again. Whenever I look down and see my wedding ring, I am reminded of the covenantal vows I made to my husband on our wedding day. I want to be as faithful to Chris as God is to me, and I know that means so much more than avoiding affairs. I need to learn what our vows mean and strive to live them out better each day.

Sir Thomas More was an invariably faithful man, not only to his work but, more importantly, to his family and to God. He showed his faithfulness to his wife and children in little ways daily. Thomas' habits reveal two main ways we can show our faithfulness to our spouses each day. First, we can work to preserve our marital intimacy through peaceful reconciliation of conflict. Second, we have to show our spouses that we prioritize them.

Preserving Intimacy

Thomas valued peace in his home and family. He set up predictable monastic-style rhythms of education, prayer, and discussion in the home. Additionally, he sought to diffuse and resolve any conflict that threatened his familial peace and intimacy. For example, when William Roper (his daughter Meg's husband) flirted with Lutheran beliefs, Thomas backed off from attacking him and just prayed for him instead.

At their wedding, a couple is bound together with a beautiful and specific intimacy. When we protect and cherish this intimacy, there is peace in the home. One way to protect our intimacy and peace is to be completely honest with our spouses, sharing our thoughts and feelings with them and listening to theirs in turn. Additionally, we can choose our battles, letting go of small things, calmly discussing larger issues, and compromising when possible.

When we inevitably fail to do one or more of these things and our marital intimacy is wounded, we can restore it with forgiveness. Sometimes, I have to forgive my husband for hurting me; other times, I have to seek his forgiveness. Both are difficult and humbling experiences! However, apologizing and forgiving are invaluable elements to any healthy relationship because they indicate a desire for reconciliation over division; for restoring marital intimacy over protecting our own pride.

Some ways to safeguard the intimacy of your marriage:

- Before you start an argument with your spouse, consider whether this is actually a big deal, or just a small complaint. If it's small, try to drop it and offer it up to God. If it's larger, find an appropriate time to talk and try to come calmly to the conversation.

- One of the best pieces of marriage advice I ever got: Be the first to say you're sorry.

- If you can't bring yourself to apologize or forgive right now, try reading Matthew 18:21-37, the parable of the unforgiving servant with the well-known command to forgive not seven but 77 times!

Prioritizing Your Spouse

Thomas More's faithful love was also evident in the personal, heartfelt letters he wrote to his wife and children almost every day. His job became increasingly demanding throughout his life, yet he continued to write to his family because he prioritized them. Each of his notes was a visible reminder of Thomas' faithful commitment to his loved ones, like Noah's rainbow or a golden wedding ring.

Your spouse will know you prioritize them when you make sacrifices out of love for them, as Abraham was willing to sacrifice Isaac for God (see Gen 22:1-19), and as God in turn was willing to sacrifice His own Son for us. Most of us will not be called to literally sacrifice our lives for our spouses, but instead to sacrifice our time, pride, and selfish interest each day. J.R.R. Tolkien asserted that faithfulness in marriage "entails...great mortification," and that no one could be a faithful spouse without "deliberate conscious exercise of the will, without self-denial."[26] This type of sacrifice might look like picking up your husband's dirty socks for the 87th time, even though you would rather not. It may mean turning off the TV during a basketball game you were looking forward to, in order to give your full attention to your wife when she has had a hard day and needs to talk.

Some ways to better prioritize your spouse:

- Carve out a time each day, even if it's only 15 minutes, for the two of you to be totally present to one another.

- Remind your spouse you love them with a quick text during the day.

- Show up — to your spouse's work party, to their art show, or just to the living room for your scheduled movie date night.

Strength and Grace

Though it may be absent from modern media, the fidelity our hearts yearn for is real and possible through Christ. The *Catechism* notes that "[Jesus] himself gives the strength and grace" to live out faithful love.[27] When we can't, He can. Trust in your own resolve, trust that your spouse will not betray you as others may have in your past, but most of all trust in God's grace abundantly gifted to you and your spouse in the Sacrament of Holy Matrimony.

Saint Thomas More is an especially good role model for those of us seeking to love God or our spouse more faithfully. He was a "courageous defender of the indissolubility of a valid ... marriage,"[28] as well as steadfast to his covenant with God. If Thomas could die rather than sign an oath that would undermine that covenant, we can recommit ourselves to the vows of the covenant we made with our spouse on our wedding day, dying the thousand tiny deaths-to-self that faithful love requires.

PRAYER

Good Lord, Give me the grace so to spend my life
that when the day of my death shall come,
though I feel pain in my body,
I may feel comfort in soul and —
with faithful hope of Your mercy,
in due love towards You and charity towards the world —
I may, through Your grace,
depart hence into Your glory.
Amen.

— From St. Thomas More's unfinished
"Treatise on the Passion" [29]

QUESTIONS FOR DISCUSSION AND REFLECTION

1. What actions can you take to solve disruptions and create peace in your household?

2. How would you define the vow to love your spouse faithfully? How did St. Thomas More live out this vow?

3. What does it mean to be faithful to God and to the Church? Has your faith ever been attacked? How did you respond?

4. We are called to be faithful to our vows even if our spouse is not. How does this compare with the covenants God made with Abraham, Noah, David, etc.?

CHAPTER 4

Loving Fruitfully:
BLESSEDS LUIGI AND
MARIA QUATTROCCHI

FEAST DAY: NOVEMBER 25

M ost people think to "love fruitfully" means to bear biological children, and this is certainly an important part of this vow. However, fruitful love also encompasses other forms of parenthood, such as adoption and spiritual parenthood, as well as witnessing the Fruits of the Holy Spirit to the world. These spiritual "fruits" will grow on the trees of our marriage if we allow the Holy Spirit to guide us in all things. There are 12: charity, joy, peace, patience, kindness, goodness, generosity, gentleness, faithfulness, modesty, self-control, and chastity.[1] Most of us can't remember all 12 of them off the top of our heads, but we can definitely see them at work in every holy marriage.

Luigi and Maria Quattrocchi are no exception. They showed they loved one another fruitfully by being open to children, and then by choosing life for their youngest even when doctors urged them to abort. Later, the Quattrocchis rejoiced when three of their four children chose religious vocations, giving us all a great example of how God can use the fruits of our love to bless the world. Maria and Luigi were also spiritual parents to many through their involvement with scouting and a plethora of other ministries, and their marriage reflected the Fruits of the Holy Spirit to everyone around them.

Let's trace the vow of fruitful love through their marriage, then look for ways that we, too, can love fruitfully.

Luigi's Birth and Childhood

Luigi Beltrame was born on Jan. 12, 1880, in Sicily. He was the third of four children born to Carlo and Francesca Beltrame. Luigi was sent to live with his childless aunt and uncle in central Italy but kept a good relationship with his biological parents and siblings. Since his uncle and aunt had effectively adopted him, Luigi added their last name to his own, and this is how he became Luigi Beltrame-Quattrocchi.

Young Luigi worked hard in his studies, first for his bachelor's degree in Ancona, and then at the University of La Sapienza in Rome, where he studied law. On the side, he enjoyed music and classic literature, interests he would share with his future wife. Luigi graduated from law school in 1902 and entered the legal service of Italy's Inland Revenue Department. Friends described Luigi as "affable, true … learned, and convinced."[2] Though he was "exceptionally virtuous," Luigi did not have a strong faith before his marriage.[3]

Maria's Birth and Childhood

Maria Corsini was born in Florence, Italy on June 24, 1884. Her family moved around frequently because her father, Angeiolo, was a captain in the Royal Army. They finally settled in Rome in 1893. Maria's mother, Giulia, was "lively and domineering;" her father was short-tempered; and this combination meant that her parents often quarreled.[4] Maria tried to be the peacekeeper in her family. Once, she even placed an olive branch on the dinner table to encourage her parents to make up after a particularly bad argument.

Maria was brought up in a much more religious family than Luigi. She attended Mass and received Communion daily, learned to recite her prayers, and attended religious counseling. She also attended parochial school for several years. Maria was "judicious, obedient, and inclined to pity" for others.[5] Though Maria was most interested in the humanities, her parents pushed her to attend business school at the Female Institute of Commerce. One beloved professor there helped Maria study Italian literature on the side, as well as to learn French and English.[6] After graduation, Maria became a lecturer and professor of education.

Meeting and Marriage

The Corsini family always enjoyed hosting social events. Luigi, a law student at the time, was occasionally invited to their parties in Rome, and befriended Maria. When both of Luigi's adoptive parents died close together, he was so grieved that he developed an intestinal ulcer and seemed close to death himself. His dear friend Maria came to his aid. She gave him a picture of the Virgin of Pompeii with some words of encouragement. Luigi recovered and carried the image and accompanying note with him for the rest of his life.

Luigi realized that he also wanted this encouraging, faithful woman by his side for life. "How grateful I am to you for the good that your love does me, that it encourages me … [you] saved my soul from skepticism," he wrote to her.[7] Luigi asked Maria to marry him on March 15, 1905, while she was playing Beethoven on the piano, and she agreed. They were married in the Basilica of Santa Maria Maggiore in Rome on Nov. 25 of that same year.

For financial reasons, Maria and Luigi started off their married life living with the Corsinis. It was a difficult arrangement: Maria's parents continued to quarrel constantly, and the house was rather full as her grandparents were also living in the home. Still, the newlyweds were determined to have a happy, virtuous marriage. Maria oversaw the couple's finances, and she made sure that they gave freely to those in need. They wrote each other long love letters, and constantly chose what was best for one another. "Their life together was a veritable contest in respect, in self-giving, in loving dependence and mutual obedience,"[8] wrote one biographer.

Choosing Life

Luigi and Maria welcomed their first child, Filippo, before their first anniversary on Oct. 15, 1906. Maria had been "used to being up-to-date with the latest in theater, music, and literature," one of her daughters wrote, so her life changed drastically when she became a mother.[9] Still, Filippo's birth brought his parents much joy. He was "a presence of God in their lives,"[10] and they were anxious to have more children. Stefania, called "Fanny," was born in March of 1908, and Cesarino arrived in November of 1909.

But the Quattrocchis' openness to life was not always a smooth, easy road. Maria struggled with severe morning sickness and other physical side effects of pregnancy, and worried that she would be unable to care for her born children during the early weeks of a new pregnancy. "Who will give me the strength to think of two children? To endure the physical and physiological exhaustion of pregnancy and the rest?" she wrote to her husband while she was pregnant with Fanny. "Believe me, I am truly in despair."[11] She pushed through her first three pregnancies, though, and in 1913 a fourth child was on the way.

Much more than the others, this was a pregnancy of "suffering and anguish."[12] Maria was diagnosed with placenta previa after many bouts of violent hemorrhaging and long periods of being bedridden. Her doctors urged her to abort the baby, giving her a survival rate of five percent or less if she chose to continue the pregnancy. At only 29 years old and with three other children to care for, Maria must have been terrified. Fanny recalled seeing her father break down in tears while speaking to a priest during this time. Still, the couple resolutely chose life for their child despite the grim prognosis.[13]

Maria was induced at eight months, and "God responded beyond all human hope."[14] Mother and child were both completely safe and healthy. Baby Enrichetta was not the only happy ending to the story, either. Through those long, uncertain months of the pregnancy, Maria and Luigi developed a "further spiritual fusion"[15] in their already beautiful marriage.

Daily Life and Habits of Faith

The Quattrocchis were a classic Italian family — noisy, active, and passionate. They enjoyed hiking and trips to the beach, like so many other families. What distinguished this family, though, was their "daily prayer, daily practice of virtue, and frequent reception of the sacraments."[16] Maria and Luigi would start their day with daily Mass together, saving their "Good morning!" until afterwards, as though their day did not really begin until they had heard God's Word and received the Eucharist. Every evening after dinner, Luigi led his family in praying the Rosary. They also had a strong familial devotion to the Sacred Heart of Jesus.

Maria and Luigi always made time for spiritual and moral growth, because they knew their own faith must be strong to raise children who appreciated everything "from the roof up," as they liked to say.[17] To this end, the parents went on retreats at a local monastery, participated in the Third Order Regular of St. Francis of Penance, and took graduate level religious courses. Their son Cesarino claimed that "there was a kind of race between Father and Mother to grow in spirituality." But this "race" did not involve any contention between the two. In fact, unlike Maria's parents, the Quattrocchis were able to resolve conflicts quietly and serenely. Enrichetta reflected, "It is obvious to think that at times they had differences of opinion, but we, their children, were never exposed to these."[18]

Children Called to Religious Vocations

The Quattrocchis were devoted parents, always inspiring joy in their children and teaching them about the love of God. "From this fertile spiritual terrain," Pope John Paul II announced at the couple's beatification Mass, "sprang vocations to the priesthood and the consecrated life."[19] Fanny became Sr. Maria Cecilia at a Benedictine convent in Milan, and later the two Quattrocchi sons left home on the exact same day in 1924 to pursue their own religious vocations. Filippo became a Benedictine, and Cesarino a Trappist monk.

Though Maria and Luigi encouraged their children to fulfill their vocations, the children's absence was still difficult for them as parents. Enrichetta recalled Luigi's "silent, discrete tears" as Fanny received her habit.[20] Once again, Maria was his strength, and the couple grew even closer to one another in the absence of their three oldest children. The Quattrocchis felt blessed to see the fruit of their marriage serving God, no matter how hard a sacrifice it was.

Professional Lives

Having children and offering them back to God in religious vocations were hardly the only visible fruits of this holy marriage. For example, Maria and Luigi both sought to help their community through their work and to offer the fruit of their professional lives to God. Luigi, who served on the boards of several banks and authorities, was hardworking and respected by his colleagues. Nevertheless, in 1943 he was blocked from a deserved position on the Counsel General of the Italian State by secular and anti-religious members of his bar association. Luigi is an "example for those who pay for their honesty and adherence to their faith by being marginalized professionally,"[21] something we see too often today. Still, he retired as an honorary deputy attorney general of the Italian State.

For her part, Maria returned to writing when her children were a bit older. This "apostolate of the pen" took off in 1920 with articles in the *Bulletin of the Italian Catholic Federation of University Students*, among other publications. Maria wrote encouraging articles on topics like marriage, family life, and education.[22]

Political Involvement and Service

Because of its underlying racism, the Quattrocchis disapproved of Italian fascism. Luigi was admonished when he refused to participate in fascist meetings, but he stood his ground. Instead, he and Maria made it their mission to get practicing Catholics back involved in Italian politics, which many were boycotting at that time. They saw an urgent need for Catholic morality to come back into play in the political arena.

The results of Italian fascism were, of course, horrible. During World War II, Maria and Luigi could not turn a blind eye to those in danger from the Nazis. They took on the great risk of storing false documents in their home to help protect their Jewish neighbors. Maria and Luigi even borrowed Benedictine robes from their sons so that they could disguise Jews and other wanted individuals and helped direct them to the safe house at the Abbey of Subiaco.[23] Maria, who had already volunteered with the Red Cross in Ethiopia during the Second Italo-Ethiopian War and in Avezzano after an earthquake in 1914, also provided medical aid in Rome during the war. After the war ended, the Quattrocchis turned their attention to the widows and people displaced by fighting or the Holocaust. They provided financial, material, and emotional support wherever they could.

Other Community Involvement

One of the movements that benefited most from the Quattrocchis' dedication was Italian scouting. Filippo and Cesarino joined their local chapter of Catholic Scouts (ASCI), and soon Luigi was their troop leader. By 1918, he was a member of the Central Commissariat for the organization. Maria, who saw God in nature, also appreciated the ascetic spirituality of the ASCI.[24] She was one of only two women at the time to take a correspondence class on the values and pedagogy of scouting, and she often welcomed her sons' troop to meet in her home.

To make scouting accessible to the less privileged boys, Luigi and his friend Gaetano founded a new troop made up mostly of street children in 1919. Luigi led this troop through 1923, and he also transferred his own sons from the "privileged" troop to this one. Luigi served as General Councilor of ASCI from 1921 until scouting was barred by fascism in 1928. The Quattrocchis' legacy lived on in the movement, though, because years later both of their sons became scouting chaplains.

The Quattrocchis served their community in several other capacities as well. They both volunteered as companions to those seeking healing at pilgrimage sites like Loreto and Lourdes through The National Italian Union for Transporting the Sick (UNITALSI). Luigi also served as Vice President of *Fronte della Famiglia* (The National Family Front), a Catholic organization that combats the breakdown of the traditional, nuclear family. Today, this same sort of work continues through The Luigi and Maria Beltrame-Quattrocchi Foundation, founded by their daughter Enrichetta in 2010. This association helps engaged and married couples cement their relationships in holiness by encouraging members to feed on the "three loaves" of the Eucharist, the Word of God, and the will of God. The Quattrocchis' community clearly benefited from the fruitfulness of their love, both during and after their lives.

Spiritual Parenthood

A couple that was so involved with their community and who lived out their faith in their daily lives so well couldn't help but attract spiritual children. Through his work, Luigi befriended many well-known political figures, some of whom were drawn into the faith despite being freemasons or even atheists before meeting him. Maria often served as a spiritual director for friends and family, especially later in life.

Rather than through preaching and chiding, the Quattrocchis won hearts for the Lord by the example of their simple, holy lives. At Luigi's funeral, a former-atheist friend approached Cesarino and Filippo. "Your father never pestered me with sermons," he told them. "But I want to tell you: It's through his life that I discovered God and that I love the Gospel. Pray for me!"[25]

Twilight Years

As the Quattrocchis grew older and their children moved out, the couple considered withdrawing to life in a monastery. They discerned that this was not God's will, but they did choose to take a vow of perfect and total openness to God that involved renouncing sexual relations and living as brother and sister after 20 years of marriage.[26] Luigi and Maria had a home built in the countryside at Seravalle, complete with a little chapel for the Blessed Sacrament. They enjoyed hiking in the Dolomite mountains, frequently accompanied by their miracle baby, Enrichetta, who had always cared for them tenderly.

On Nov. 9, 1951, at age 71, Luigi died after a heart attack. Upon his death, Maria became more devoted to the Mass than ever, because she felt Luigi's presence there. "Little by little, he is present to me ever more, most of all in prayer, at Communion, before the altar," she wrote a few months after his death.[27] Maria also recommitted herself to her writing at this time, publishing her most famous book *Radiografia de un matrimonio* ("X-Ray of a Marriage"), which reflected on her own beautiful union with Luigi. At age 81, Maria also suffered a heart attack and died in Enrichetta's arms on Aug. 21, 1965.

Beatification and Legacy

Luigi and Maria Beltrame-Quattrocchi were the first married couple ever to be beatified together. The Mass of beatification took place on Oct. 21, 2001, the 20-year anniversary of the publication of *Familiaris consortio,* a papal encyclical about the role of the family in the Church and in the world. As only Fanny had died at that point, Enrichetta (aged 87) was in the congregation to witness her parents becoming Blesseds, and both Filippo (aged 95) and Cesarino (aged 91) were able to concelebrate Mass with the Pope!

The Quattrocchis show us all that marriage is not only a path to Heaven for the spouses, but that parents set the example for their children to become saintly. Certainly, the Quattrocchis' children were set on the right path. Both of their sons were known for exceptional gifts of preaching and working on behalf of others. Cesarino even won the Silver Medal for Military Valor after risking his life as a military chaplain in World War II. Fanny was a beloved nun, and in 2018, little Enrichetta's own case for beatification was opened!

A cardinal responsible for causes of sainthood notes that the Quattrocchis "made a true domestic church of their family, which was open to life, to prayer, to the social apostolate, to solidarity with the poor and to friendship."[28] Their story has been shared in articles, books, and even a musical-theatre program called "A Halo for Two," which is an inspiring story full of ways to live out the vow to love our spouses fruitfully. To highlight their call to sainthood through marital love, the Quattrocchis' remains were moved to the Church of Our Lady of Divine Love after their beatification. Their feast day is celebrated on their wedding anniversary, Nov. 25.

Marital Vow: Loving Fruitfully

Biological Parenthood and NFP

Maria struggled with the side effects of all her pregnancies, and her fourth pregnancy was actually life-threatening. Nevertheless, she and Luigi chose to trust in God and continued to be open to life in their marriage. Enrichetta, their little miracle, became a wonderful blessing to her parents, staying by their side and serving them in their old age. The Quattrocchis' other three children all chose religious vocations, and in this way the fruits of their blessed marriage came back to bless them and overflowed to bless the whole Church.

Most married couples are also called to love fruitfully through biological parenthood. The very first commandment God gives to His people in the Bible is "Be fertile and multiply" (Gen 1:28). The story of creation did not end in Genesis, but is instead ongoing, as God allows parents to cooperate with Him in creating new life.[29] *Humanae vitae* attests that "[c]hildren are really the supreme gift of marriage,"[30] and that the sexual act is naturally ordered toward the conception of new life. To preserve the fruitfulness of our love, then, no sexual act can be closed to life.

Catholics believe that using any form of contraception negates "the spousal meaning of the body and the call to be selflessly creative."[31] However, the Church does recognize that we must balance openness to life with responsible parenthood. Instead of contraception, we can choose to use Natural Family Planning.

Natural Family Planning (NFP) refers to a wide umbrella of scientifically-developed methods whereby couples observe and chart the natural signs of a woman's fertility in order to decide when to have sex. NFP is not contraceptive, because no barrier, pill, herb, or device is used to prevent conception in any sexual act. Instead, couples who practice NFP work with the God-created cycles of a woman's fertility. A couple choosing to postpone pregnancy for the time being can choose to practice chastity (a fruit of the Spirit!) on fertile days. This periodic self-control "signifies spiritual energy capable of defending love from the perils of selfishness."[32]

I can attest that, in my own marriage, practicing NFP has forced Chris and me to learn how to show our love for one another in non-sexual ways. NFP has also made us both appreciate more deeply how "fearfully and wonderfully" God has made our male and female bodies. NFP has helped us both avoid and achieve pregnancy in different seasons of our marriage. Resources for popular methods of NFP like Marquette, Creighton, and Billings are available online for anyone interested in learning more about protecting the fruitfulness of their marriage covenant.

Some ways to incorporate these teachings into your marriage:

- If you have any questions or doubts about Catholic teaching on sexual unity or contraception, I cannot recommend highly enough that you read *Humanae vitae*, a beautiful and concise papal encyclical available for free online.

- Research one of the above NFP methods online together with your spouse.

- If you already have children, thank God for blessing you with them, and ask Him to bless the world through them in turn.

Other Forms of Parenthood

Of course, there are also married couples that are unable to conceive children. Some may be past the age of fertility, and some, for whatever reason, carry the heavy cross of infertility. Infertile couples are by no means unable to love fruitfully, because "love *always* bears fruit."[33] The fruits of such a marriage may instead be adopted children, a beautiful choice we see at work in Luigi Beltrame-Quattrochi's life as he was adopted by his uncle and aunt. You may also choose to foster children. The Quattrocchis briefly fostered an 18-day-old baby girl whose parents had died of the Spanish Flu. In any case, you and your spouse are called to have spiritual children, people of all ages who look to you as role models in the faith. The Quattrocchis had heaps of these, too!

Sex does not exist only for procreation — it is equally ordered to the unity of the spouses. A couple past the age of fertility or facing infertility remains ordained to "the expression and strengthening" of their union through sex while still being open to life if it were possible.[34] Whether you are able to conceive or not, enjoy the gift God has given us in the marital embrace!

Ways to incorporate other forms of parenthood into your marriage:

- Whether or not you are able to conceive, discuss with your spouse whether adoption or foster parenthood is right for you.

- Prayerfully discern who in your life might think of you as a spiritual parent. Consider how you might be a better example to that person.

- If you and your spouse are unable to conceive, pray that God would still help you embrace the gift of sexual unity in your marriage.

The Fruits of the Spirit in Your Marriage

Whether you have biological, adopted, foster, or spiritual children in your family, "the family is the first school of those social virtues which every society needs."[35] This means that you are called to witness the Fruits of the Holy Spirit to your spouse and to your children, because this fruitfulness will then overflow from your family out into the world.

Here, again, are the Fruits of the Holy Spirit: charity, joy, peace, patience, kindness, goodness, generosity, gentleness, faithfulness, modesty, self-control, and chastity. Twelve beautiful fruits observable in the lives of all holy people, and in all holy marriages, too. For example, Luigi and Maria showed the fruit of charity by volunteering almost all their free time to scouting, the Red Cross, and many other organizations. The fruits of peace and joy were also evident to their children, who described the general atmosphere in the home as "supernatural, serene, and happy."[36]

A few ways to foster gifts of the Holy Spirit in your marriage:

- Find a quiet 15 minutes to turn your phones off, light a candle, and pray the Rosary together. This will foster peace and faith, if not others!

- The next time you feel irritated with your spouse, pause for a moment, and think about how you could respond with more patience or gentleness.

- Try this simple but powerful prayer: "Come, Holy Spirit, by the grace of my Confirmation, bring me self-control." Or insert any other gift you need in the moment!

To the Heights of Holiness

The Quattrocchis welcomed children, even when it was physically and emotionally difficult for them, but their fruitfulness didn't end there. They inspired hundreds of spiritual children through the countless hours they devoted to ministry, from the scouting movement to the Red Cross. They also demonstrated the Fruits of the Holy Spirit in their daily lives, especially charity, joy, and faith. In the Gospel of Matthew, Jesus tells us "By their fruits you will know them ... [E]very good tree bears good fruit" (Mt 7:16-17). This holy marriage is easily recognized by its varied and beautiful fruits.

Here is a prayer by the Association of Maria and Luigi Beltrame-Quattrocchi, which reminds us to recognize the "divine gift" of our fertility, to find joy in our (biological, adoptive, foster, or spiritual) parenthood, and to love fruitfully all the way to the "heights of holiness" to which we, like the Quattrocchis, are all called.

PRAYER

Lord Jesus, you called Luigi and Maria,
spouses and parents according to Your Heart,
to live day after day,
in constant fidelity to you in daily life.
You who with your presence
have sanctified the dwellings of Nazareth, Cana,
and Bethany, giving families the seal of the love
of the Father, the Son and the Holy Spirit,
grant that their witness and intercession may contribute,
with the help of the Mother in heaven,
to consolidate the journey of faith and love
begun at the foot of the altar;
to pervade with Your presence the young couples
filling their jars with You;
to open them gratefully to the divine gift of fertility,
happy with the vocation
to motherhood and fatherhood in the image
of God the father and mother;
to dedicate themselves with joy and commitment
to the education of children,
future citizens of Heaven; to share the sufferings
of families in difficulty
and accompany them on the path of love for You,
who are Love; to make sufferings
precious opportunities to mature and love more.
Grant us to strive without compromise
to the heights of holiness to which you have called
each of us from eternity. Amen.

— *"Concluding Prayer" of the Association Maria*
and Luigi Beltrame-Quattrocchi[37]

QUESTIONS FOR DISCUSSION AND REFLECTION

1. After reading this chapter, how would you define "loving fruitfully"? How did Bls. Luigi and Maria live out this vow?

2. Generosity is one of the 12 Fruits of the Holy Spirit. Where do you see this fruit in the Quattrocchis' lives and in their marriage? How could you foster generosity in your own marriage?

3. Before reading this chapter, had you ever heard of Natural Family Planning (NFP)? What questions or concerns do you have about NFP? Who or what might be a helpful resource as you continue learning more?

4. In what ways is parenthood (of any kind!) exciting to you? In what ways is it overwhelming?

5. Who is a spiritual parent to you? What makes them inspirational or encouraging to you? How could you emulate them to your own spiritual children one day?

CHAPTER 5

For Better, for Worse:
SAINTS ELIZABETH AND ZECHARIAH
FEAST DAY: NOVEMBER 5

I generally don't reflect on my vows to love Chris "for richer or for poorer" or "in sickness and in health" on a daily basis. But this vow, "for better or for worse," sometimes spoken as "in good times, in bad times" — well, that's all the "times." That's all day, every day. That's our whole marriage.

Saints Elizabeth and Zechariah, parents of St. John the Baptist, certainly lived through some better times and some worse times. All the authoritative information we have about these saints can be found in just the first chapter of the Gospel of Luke, but in that one chapter we watch the couple experience both crushing lows and soaring highs. They carried the cross of infertility for decades, far past the glimmer of hope that may remain during normal childbearing years. Suddenly, though, the couple was blessed with a child in their old age — a child announced by an angel, filled with the Holy Spirit, and given the mission to prepare the way of the Messiah! They spent several months with Mary, the Mother of God, and her unborn Child. Saints Elizabeth and Zechariah were given the privilege of being both the parents of a great prophet and saint, and relatives of Jesus Himself.

Elizabeth and Zechariah offered their suffering and their rejoicing, their "for better" and their "for worse" to God. Through it all, they remained a holy and righteous couple that can help us learn to live out this important vow, too.

Ancestry and Background

Elizabeth and Zechariah lived in the "hill country" of Judah (Lk 1:39). They were both from the tribe of Levi and descended from Aaron, the brother of Moses. God had set the tribe of Levi apart to perform priestly duties such as bearing the Ark of the Covenant (Dt 10:8), and Aaron had served as the first high priest of the Israelites (Ex 28:1). Following this heritage, Zechariah served as a priest in the Jerusalem Temple. His wife, Elizabeth, was "kinswoman" to the Virgin Mary. Some translations call Elizabeth and Mary cousins, but they may have been more distant than first cousins. It is also possible Elizabeth was Mary's aunt. Elizabeth, who was past normal childbearing age when the events of the Gospel unfolded, was certainly much older than Mary, thought to be a young teenager.

Infertility

One of the only other pieces of background information Luke gives us about this couple is that they were childless. Infertility would have caused the same aching, longing, and pain as it does today, but there would have been an added layer of shame in those days. The ancient law plainly states that those who follow the rules and remain in God's favor will not experience sterility (Dt 7:14), so it was assumed that all childless couples had not lived by the law. Infertility was generally blamed on the woman, so Elizabeth probably felt particularly ashamed, but Zechariah, who was held to a higher moral standard as a priest, would also have suffered. They almost certainly would have experienced some degree of exclusion or distrust from their community.[1]

The evangelist Luke, however, affirms this couple was "righteous in the eyes of God, observing all the commandments and ordinances of the Lord blamelessly" (Lk 1:6). Luke is quick to praise Zechariah and Elizabeth precisely because his contemporary readers would have otherwise assumed they were sinful and cursed.

Angelic Messenger

Child or no child, life marched on. Zechariah, for his part, continued in his priestly role, which in those days only entailed a week of service at a time, twice a year. One of these periods of service arrived, and he headed to the Temple, where he would live in the priestly chambers throughout the week. The assembled priests drew lots each day to determine who would offer incense during daily worship. This was the holiest of tasks, "an honour which no priest could enjoy more than once during his lifetime."[2]

One fateful day, it was Zechariah's turn. The whole congregation waited while Zechariah went in to offer incense at the holy altar. He should have finished the task quickly, then emerged to lead them all in prayer. Instead, Zechariah was gone for a long time and when he came out, he was unable to speak. Everyone knew something extraordinary had happened during the offering, but what?

Luke tells us that the angel Gabriel had appeared to Zechariah at the altar. Gabriel told Zechariah that his prayers for a child had been heard by God: his wife would bear a son, and they should name him John. Zechariah responded with great doubt and asked for proof this would really happen. "How shall I know this?" he asked the angel. "For I am an old man, and my wife is advanced in years" (Lk 1:18). As Ferdinand Holböck reflects, Zechariah's lack of faith here is "astounding": this was a message from an angel to a priest, in one of the holiest places in the Temple. He had every reason to believe the message, but apparently, he needed more.[3] Because of his doubt, Zechariah was struck mute until after his son was born and named.

Elizabeth received the news about her own seemingly impossible pregnancy not from an angel in a Temple, but through interpretating the clumsy signs of her suddenly mute husband. Nevertheless, she responded with much more faith than Zechariah. She acknowledged with joy that God had blessed her with a child "to take away my disgrace before others" (Lk 1:25). Elizabeth decided to hide herself away for the first five months of her pregnancy in silent retreat. After this, in her sixth month of pregnancy, Elizabeth was visited by her young kinswoman, Mary, who was also miraculously pregnant.

The Visitation of Mary and Birth of John the Baptist

"Most blessed are you among women, and blessed is the fruit of your womb." Elizabeth greeted Mary with words that have become very familiar to Catholics. "And how does this happen to me," she continued, "that the mother of my Lord should come to me?" (Lk 1:42-43) Though the angel Gabriel had told Mary about Elizabeth's pregnancy, we have no reason to believe that Elizabeth knew about Mary's pregnancy, much less that Mary's unborn child was the Son of God. Elizabeth speaks in a "prophetic voice"[4] when she confesses Mary's child as her Lord, which must have encouraged Mary greatly. Elizabeth also reveals that her own unborn child had "leaped" in her womb at Mary's greeting, fulfilling Gabriel's word that the baby would be "filled with the holy Spirit" even before his birth (Lk 1:41).

Mary remained with her relatives from the sixth to the ninth month of Elizabeth's pregnancy, meaning she may have been present for the birth of John. I can imagine that Elizabeth appreciated the company, especially with Zechariah being mute the whole time. These kinswomen were both dealing with miraculous pregnancies announced by angels and misunderstood by society, and they were preparing to welcome sons who would grow up to be two of the most influential people to ever live. Mary and Elizabeth had a lot in common with one another at a time when they had little in common with others. From the Visitation, as Mary's stay is called in the Joyful Mysteries of the Rosary, we can also "look for opportunities to give others a reason to praise God."[5] After Elizabeth identified Mary as the "blessed" Mother of the Lord, Mary uttered the beautiful prayer we now call the Magnificat: "My soul proclaims the greatness of the Lord; my spirit rejoices in God my savior. ..." (Lk 1:46-47).

Finally, Elizabeth gave birth to her son. Others assumed this child would be named after his father, but Elizabeth told them that he would be named John, as the angel had prescribed. Zechariah confirmed this by writing on a tablet, and "[i]mmediately his mouth was opened, his tongue freed, and he spoke blessing God" (Lk 1:64). Zechariah had learned his lesson. His doubt had been replaced by faith in the God who had blessed Elizabeth and him with a son who would "go before the Lord to prepare his ways," and who had also blessed Mary and the whole world with a Son who would bring "redemption to his people" (Lk 1:76, 68).

The name John means "the Lord is gracious,"[6] and this must have resonated with Elizabeth and Zechariah in this moment. After so many years of longing for a child and bearing the cultural shame of infertility, their "neighbors and relatives heard that the Lord had shown his great mercy toward [them], and they rejoiced with [them]" (Lk 1:58). They had even more reason to rejoice, knowing a few months later their relative Mary would also deliver her Son, Jesus the Messiah.

Elizabeth and Zechariah's Later Years

Elizabeth and Zechariah were already advanced in years when John was born, but at least one of them may have had their life cut short by martyrdom. In Matthew 23:35, we hear that a "righteous" man, Zechariah, son of Barachiah, was "murdered between the sanctuary and the altar." Given the names and the location of the murder (in the Temple), it is very possible that this is the same Zechariah we met in this chapter. Some believe that Zechariah was killed for not disclosing the whereabouts of his young son John during the "murder of the innocents," when Herod tried to eliminate the threat of the prophesied Messiah by killing all local baby boys.[7] Saint Gregory of Nyssa holds that Zechariah was actually martyred for acknowledging Jesus' divinity and Mary's virgin birth. Regardless of the specific reason, it seems likely that Zechariah was martyred. In 2003, excavators found an inscription in a fourth-century tomb that reads, "This is the tomb of Zachariah, the martyr, the holy priest, the father of John." Based on these stories, Zechariah may have reversed the doubt he had shown in that same Temple at Gabriel's message, showing faith and strength even to death.[8]

What happened to Elizabeth and baby John after Zechariah's death? The Orthodox claim that Elizabeth fled the pursuers of the Holy Innocents with her baby. When she begged God for safety, a "hill opened up and concealed her and the infant."[9] Then, Elizabeth allegedly died forty days after her husband (of old age, or was she also martyred?) and the infant John was provided for by God Himself. We do know from the Gospels that John the Baptist "became strong in spirit" and stayed in the desert until he began his ministry. He would eventually emerge to baptize people in the Jordan, including Jesus Himself. In this moment, John would also reveal Jesus as the Messiah, and encourage his own disciples to become Jesus' disciples instead.[10]

Patronage and Legacy

Throughout their decades of longing for a child and shame of childlessness, Elizabeth and Zechariah lived holy lives. As soon as Elizabeth heard the angel's message, she believed that "nothing will be impossible for God" (Lk 1:37), and she thanked Him for blessing her. She inspired Mary to glorify God with the beautiful words of the Magnificat, and she helped her husband move from doubt towards the deep conviction of a martyr. Though it is unclear how long Elizabeth and Zechariah lived after John's birth, these holy parents certainly set him on the path towards his important ministry by their example.

For these reasons, Sts. Elizabeth and Zechariah are honored by people of many faith traditions, including Greek

Orthodox and Eastern Orthodox Catholics, Anglicans, Lutherans, and even Muslims. Roman Catholics honor them on their shared feast day of Nov. 5.

Marital Vow: For Better, For Worse

During their years of infertility, Elizabeth and Zechariah surely leaned on one another and also on God. Their suffering was real, but it was not in vain because they offered it to God and let Him use it to make them holy. Later, when their son John was born, they rejoiced together! In this moment, they offered their joy and thanksgiving to God. In each season of life, they gave God whatever they had to give — tears or songs, aching or celebration. We can do the same in our marriages to live out the vow to love our spouse "for better or for worse."

Leaning On and Appreciating One Another

One of the parts of marriage I find most beautiful is knowing that Chris and I will be there for one another in seasons of doubt, sorrow, and pain. I was there with him, holding his hand, when he said goodbye to his grandmother for the last time. I cried on his shoulder too many evenings to count when I was struggling as a teacher. Sorrow shared, as they say, is sorrow halved, and I know these moments supporting one another strengthened our bond. These moments also made me better appreciate some of Chris' qualities, such as his listening skills and his stability.

Seasons of emptiness or sadness can also help us appreciate seasons of joy. We can see this in Elizabeth and Zechariah's pure joy at welcoming their son after so many years of longing. It is also evident in the Church's liturgical calendar: Easter is all the sweeter after a long, penitential Lent. I personally know I will never take a good night of sleep for granted again after the weeks and months of sleeplessness I've had with my babies!

Some ways to lean on and appreciate your spouse during times of suffering:

- Start a new tradition to help your family understand the importance of the liturgical seasons. In Advent, for example, my family adds an ornament to our Jesse Tree each day and reads the associated scripture to prepare for Jesus' birth. This preparation will make Christmas even more joyful!

- If you are in a tough season of marriage, look through some photos from a happier time, such as your wedding day or the birth of a child.

- If you are in a joyful season of marriage, think back on trials you two have weathered together. Thank God for getting you through these times.

Growing In Virtue

Though we sometimes wish God would just bestow virtue upon us on request, He often seems to instead give us more opportunities to practice and hone the virtues we desire. When I pray that God would grant me more patience with my husband when he leaves dirty socks on the ground, it seems there are suddenly even more socks! Deeper suffering than my frustrations with socks can ultimately correspond to much more growth in virtue. Consider, for example, the awesome patience of couples that have raised children with special needs.

Suffering has been compared to the painful treatment of chemotherapy to kill cancer. When we are oblivious to our own lack of virtue, we might feel God is needlessly torturing us with trials. In reality, God is trying to remove the most dangerous cancers of all — selfishness, pride, sin — because He wants us to live forever with Him in Heaven.[11] Let God use your suffering to make you a better Christian and a better spouse!

Ways to foster growth in virtue during times of suffering:

- Think of a trial you are currently facing in your marriage, no matter how trivial. Ask God in prayer how He might be using this to help you grow in virtue.

- Ask your spouse what is causing suffering in his or her life. Brainstorm ways you could support your spouse through this suffering, growing in kindness and charity in the process.

- The next time you feel frustrated with your spouse, try this short prayer: "God, by the grace of my marriage, give me patience with my spouse." Then be prepared for more opportunities to *practice* patience, reinforced by God's grace (power)!

Offering Up Suffering

While most of the world fears and hates suffering, the Catholic Church teaches that our suffering can be meaningful, meritorious, and even sweet when we offer it to God. Jesus told His disciples to take up their crosses and follow Him (Mt 16:24). When we embrace the idea of suffering under the unique crosses of our lives, we are imitating Christ and following in His footsteps, which lead straight to Heaven. Furthermore, if you lay it at the foot of the Cross and give it to Him, Christ will gladly receive, redeem, and make use of your gift of suffering.

This side of Heaven, the question is not *whether* you will suffer, but *how* you will choose to suffer. Consider the two thieves who were crucified on either side of Jesus. These two men suffered the exact same physical pain. However, one accepted his suffering and cried out to Jesus to remember him when He came into His kingdom (Lk 23:42), while the other hated his suffering and insulted Jesus. This second thief died miserable and unrepentant, and we can have no assurance at all that he chose Christ and eternal life. Meanwhile, Jesus promised the "good thief," "Amen, I say to you, today you will be with me in Paradise" (Lk 23:43). I can only imagine these words brought the man peace before his death. We can take Jesus at His word that St. Dismas, as we now know him, is in Paradise.

Some ways to offer up suffering in tough times:

- Try this simple prayer: "God, may Your will be done in my life. Please be with me through this suffering and use it for Your glory."

- Ask for the intercession of St. Dismas to help you accept the crosses and suffering in your life.

- Make a sacrifice on your spouse's behalf. Temporarily give up sweets, TV, or some other treat, with the intention that some suffering in their life would cease, or that they would repent of sin.

Rejoice and Be Glad!

Of course, there will also be times of celebration and joy within your marriage, from the early "honeymoon stage" to anniversaries, birthdays, and vacations. I also love celebrating Chris' accomplishments, like when he was promoted last fall or when he completes a beautiful painting. I know he will always be my cheerleader when I successfully potty-train one of our toddlers or when I finish a chapter of this book.

To complete the idiom I referenced earlier, joy shared certainly is joy doubled, especially in a marriage. You and your spouse are one flesh in your covenant, so your spouse's joy really is your joy, too! When the two of you are celebrating, be sure to offer your joy to God just as you would offer your suffering. God can use that, too — for example, to attract those around you to a Christ-centered life.

Some ways to incorporate these points in the joyful seasons of your marriage:

- Think of a new tradition to use in celebrating your next family/marriage milestone. This could be as small as having cupcakes for a birthday, or as big as planning a trip!
- Try a simple prayer like this: "Thank you, God for the blessings you have bestowed on me and my family. Please accept the gift of my grateful heart. Please use my joy to bring others to you!"

Whatever You Have

Elizabeth and Zechariah had some higher highs and lower lows than most of us will, and they offered them all to God. When they suffered from infertility and societal shame, they offered God their pain. When they hosted Mary and their unborn Savior for three months, they offered God thanksgiving and praise. And once He arrived, they even offered up their own precious son, John, to prepare the way for God's Son, Jesus. Whatever you have to give today, give it up to God: praise, tears, songs of joy, or a broken heart. Whether you are in a "for better" or a "for worse" period, Jesus can redeem it and use it if you offer it to Him.

Here is part of the "Canticle of Zechariah." These are the first words Zechariah spoke once he was no longer mute, when he was "filled with the Holy Spirit" (Lk 1:67). This famous prayer is a great example of giving glory to God, who brings dawn to all our darkness.

PRAYER

Blessed be the Lord, the God of Israel,
for he has visited and brought redemption to his people.
He has raised up a horn for our salvation
within the house of David his servant,
even as he promised through the mouth
of his holy prophets from of old:
salvation from our enemies and from
the hand of all who hate us,
to show mercy to our fathers and to be mindful of his holy
covenant and of the oath he swore to Abraham our father,
and to grant us that, rescued from the hand of enemies,
without fear we might worship him in holiness and
righteousness before him all our days.
And you, child, will be called prophet of the Most High,
for you will go before the Lord to prepare his ways,
to give his people knowledge of salvation through
the forgiveness of their sins,
because of the tender mercy of our God
by which the daybreak from on high will visit us to shine on
those who sit in darkness and death's shadow,
to guide our feet into the path of peace.

— *From "The Canticle of Zechariah," Lk 1:68-79*

QUESTIONS FOR DISCUSSION AND REFLECTION

1. What does it mean to love your spouse "for better or for worse"? How did Sts. Elizabeth and Zechariah show this?

2. Which of your spouse's qualities make him or her a great support system in tough times? How can you show you appreciate these qualities?

3. What does it mean to unite your suffering with Jesus' suffering? How can you offer Him your suffering?

4. Do you feel that your spouse's joy is really your joy, too? What are some ways you could show your spouse you are rejoicing with them and being their cheerleader?

CHAPTER 6

For Richer, for Poorer:
BLESSED KARL I OF AUSTRIA
AND SERVANT OF GOD ZITA

FEAST DAY: OCTOBER 21

When my husband Chris and I vowed to love one another "for richer or for poorer" up on the altar, it didn't take too much thought. We were young and in love, focused more on the details of our wedding day than on the details of our budget as a married couple. Also, we are both blessed to have grown up in well-off families. Our parents were always ready to serve as a safety net if we needed them, so we had never worried too much about our financial future, anyway. Maybe you are in a similar boat.

But life throws curveballs all the time. What if Chris were gravely injured tomorrow, rendered unable to work indefinitely? What if we found out that God had decided to bless us with triplets? It could happen.

Around 22 percent of divorces and breakups are linked to financial issues.[1] Problems with money can be overwhelming and can cause a lot of blaming and bitterness in a marriage. Even if you are blessed to be financially stable right now, the vow to love your spouse "for richer or for poorer" is still relevant, because you can learn how to love in this season of "for richer," and prepare for any curveballs that might come later on in life. To live out this vow, we can learn how to navigate any financial conflicts and to remain as committed to our marriage in rags as we are in riches.

I can't think of any better example than wealthy world leaders who suddenly became penniless exiles. Blessed Karl I and his wife, the Servant of God Zita of Bourbon-Parma, were the last emperor and empress of the Austro-Hungarian Empire. Though their home and lifestyle changed drastically after their political exile, their strong, holy marriage did not.

Karl and Zita's Early Years

Karl of the House of Austria was born near Vienna, Austria on Aug. 17, 1887. The current emperor, Kaiser Franz Josef, was Karl's great uncle, so Karl was born into royalty, but was not in the immediate line of succession to the throne. Like most royals of the day, Karl was given quite a mouthful for a full name: Karl Franz Josef Ludwig Hubert Georg Otto Maria von Habsburg-Lothringen. In many sources, his first name is anglicized to Charles. I will stick with the Austrian spelling of Karl here because being Austrian was particularly important to this holy man.

Karl was consistently described as an honest, cheerful child with a heart for the poor. He did chores for family members just to earn small coins that he could donate and went on to grow a garden of fruits and vegetables for the hungry. Karl's tutor wrote that Karl's "greatest joy was in being allowed to be an altar-boy." Religion was an important part of Karl's upbringing because his mother was a strong Catholic. She took him to daily Mass and made sure that he frequently received the Sacraments.[2]

Princess Zita of Bourbon-Parma was born on May 9, 1892, in Parma, Italy. She was given a name to rival her future husband's: Zita Maria delle Grazie Adelgonda Micaela Raffaela Gabriella Giuseppina Antonia Luisa Agnese. Zita was named after the patron saint of domestic workers. Such a name seemed like an odd choice for a princess, but it ended up being perfect for a woman who saw charitable deeds as "part of her religion," just like St. Zita.[3]

Zita's father, Duke Robert of Bourbon-Parma, had 12 children with his first wife. When she died, he married Zita's mother, Maria Antonia, daughter to the former king of Portugal, and had 12 more children. Even though three of these children died young, Zita grew up with no fewer than 20 siblings! Karl and his singular brother, Max, visited the Bourbon-Parma family on occasion, and Karl enjoyed having so many children around. He would be reunited with his childhood friend Zita as a young adult.

Zita descended from two of the most important Catholic families in Europe: the French Bourbons and the royal family of Portugal. Zita's father and his first wife had the exceedingly rare honor of being married by the Pope himself! As a child, Zita studied and grew in faith at a contemplative convent in England where her grandmother was serving as abbess. Three of Zita's sisters eventually became nuns there, and Zita prayerfully discerned this vocation as well. Ultimately, she realized she was not called to be a nun. In 1909, Zita finished her schooling and headed home to Italy, eager to find out what God had planned for her instead.

Engagement and Marriage

Karl was reintroduced to Zita in 1910 when he was stationed with the military near the family she was visiting in Bohemia. The two were "glad to meet again and became close friends," Zita wrote. She slowly grew to have romantic feelings for him but claimed that Karl "seemed to have made up his mind much more quickly." In the photos announcing their engagement on June 13, 1911, the couple looked "unpretentiously happy."[4]

Before the wedding, Pope (now St.) Pius X invited Zita and a few family members to the Vatican for a private audience. Karl and Zita's marriage was important for the future of the Catholic Church in Europe. The Holy Father congratulated Zita on her engagement to the man he saw as "a gift from Heaven for what Austria has done for the Church." He then foretold that Karl would "soon" be on the throne, though there were still two healthy men in line before him.[5] The words of the Pope's eerie prediction would ring in Zita's ears when Karl became emperor just five years later.

Karl and Zita were married on Oct. 21, 1911, in one of the earliest ceremonies ever recorded on film. The couple's vows were "clear ... emphatic and joyous." The engraving on the inside of their rings read, "*Sub tuum praesidium confugimus, sancta Dei genitrix*" ("Under your protection and umbrella, we flee, Holy Mother of God").[6] Karl told his bride, "Now we must help each other to get to Heaven."[7] Karl and Zita started their journey to Heaven together by praying at the shrine of Our Lady at Mariazell during their honeymoon.

Karl and Zita had "the same deep faith, the same simple tastes, the same love of home and ... the same sense of humour."[8] Their personalities were different but complementary: She was extroverted and passionate, while he was quiet and introspective. Zita was very respectful of Karl's authority, but she was well educated herself and more decisive than he was, so Karl often sought her counsel. Above all, they shared a commitment to serving God and growing in virtue.

Parenthood

The Habsburg family grew quickly. Karl and Zita's first baby, Crown Prince Otto (followed by plenty of other names!) was born just after their first anniversary in November 1912. Karl and Zita eventually had eight children together, through extremely varied circumstances. By the time the last child, Elisabeth, was born, Karl had died, and Zita was living in exile, penniless and scared. Still, despite the challenges they endured, Karl and Zita remained admirably open to life throughout their marriage.

Zita was a loving and attentive mother, and Karl always managed to find at least a few minutes to spend with his children, even during 18-hour workdays as emperor. The "extremely careful" investigation into Karl's family life for his beatification concluded that he was a devoted father and committed to his children's upbringing in faith and morality.[9] The Habsburgs often personally catechized their children, especially when the family had to travel.

Habits of Faith

Karl and Zita established habits of faith for their family including praying the Rosary, attending daily Mass, and reading and discussing Scripture together. These habits stuck, no matter their life circumstances. For example, Karl attended Mass in the field during his military service, and he and Zita even begged for the opportunity to receive the Eucharist while en route to their exile, when so much else must have been on their minds.

The family also continued some Habsburg traditions of *Pietas Austriaca* ("Austrian Piety"), which dated back to the medieval period. Some of these included washing the feet of the elderly in imitation of Christ at the Last Supper, and joining the annual Corpus Christi procession to honor the Eucharist. *Pietas Austriaca* traditions helped the Habsburg family to see their political positions through Catholic eyes and to rule benevolently following the example of true Christian leaders like King Rudolf I (1218-1291).[10]

Karl Becomes Emperor

When Karl was born, his great-uncle Franz Josef was the emperor. Preceding Karl in line for the throne was Franz Josef's son, Rudolph, followed by another great-uncle, Maximilian; his grandfather, Karl Ludwig; his uncle, Franz Ferdinand; and his father, Otto. Rudolph and Maximilian both died under unfortunate circumstances and without heirs. Franz Ferdinand had signed away his children's rights to the throne when he married beneath him.[11] Karl's father, Otto, had already died when Franz Ferdinand was assassinated in 1914, effectively starting World War I. Just two years later, current emperor

Franz Josef died after 68 years of ruling Austria-Hungary. And so, Karl became the emperor of the double monarchy at age 29 in 1916. Zita was just 24.

Because Karl was so far removed from the throne as a child, his father had not seen a need for him to study statecraft. However, despite his lack of experience and training, Karl had big plans for his reign. First, he sought to create a strong welfare system to serve his people. Second, Karl wanted to restructure his diverse empire peacefully along federalist lines, creating a sort of United States of Greater Austria. Finally, and above all else, Karl thirsted for peace during an era in which every country in Europe appeared to be ready to take up arms next to an ally or against an enemy for the smallest reason.

In his coronation oath, Karl pledged first and foremost to be the servant of his people. He was inspired by the principles of Catholic kingship, and particularly by Pope Leo XIII's 1891 encyclical *Rerum Novarum* to create new social security and welfare systems.[12] Though some among his court mocked his efforts, Karl "donated much of his private fortune" and sent his imperial carriages to deliver coal to the poor shivering in the cold during the war.[13] He also established policies like rent control, child and youth protection, family rights, industrial law, and employee welfare. Many of these structures are still in place in Austria today.[14]

Karl saw conflict brewing between the many ethnic groups in his empire, and he had a peaceful solution. He could restructure the empire, allowing each territory some legal autonomy while uniting all the states under one economy and one national defense. Karl believed that if these initiatives failed, each ethnic nation would be left vulnerable. Unfortunately, Karl was unable to garner the necessary support for his plans, and his predictions came true: his empire was dismantled after the war, and various states succumbed to civil unrest, German Nazism, or Soviet Communism.

Peace Emperor

Karl was not yet emperor when Austria-Hungary found itself pressured into the Great War. In his first declaration as emperor, Karl pledged to win back "the sorely-missed blessing of peace" for his people as soon as possible.[15] He especially hated war after his own frontline experience and, almost singularly among world leaders at the time, he truly desired to enact Pope Benedict XV's proposed initiatives for peace. Karl opposed German attacks on neutral ships and civilian bombing, calling both "inhumane." His people called him the *Friedenskaiser* — the "Peace Emperor."[16]

As the carnage raged on, it became apparent to Karl (but not to his ally, Kaiser Wilhelm of Germany) that the Central European Powers would lose not only untold numbers of young men, but the Great War itself. Karl tried to convince Wilhelm to negotiate peace with the Allies; this proved hopeless. Next, Karl tried to negotiate a separate peace for Austria-Hungary. The "Sixtus Affair" was complicated by many factors, and ultimately, a separate peace was not achieved, countless more Austrian lives were lost, and Karl's reputation was greatly marred in the eyes of both Germany and the Allied forces.[17]

After the War

When the war ended, there was unrest in the empire and talk of dissolving the monarchy. Karl refused to abdicate, but not out of pride or selfishness: He believed God had entrusted to him the protection of the people of the empire. Abdication might mean leaving each ethnic state to fend for itself, and this chaos was to be avoided at all costs. In November 1918, Karl withdrew from power temporarily because he was led to believe that the people of his empire would be allowed to vote and peacefully choose the form of government they preferred. Unfortunately, this national vote never actually took place. During this time, Karl and his family were obliged to seek safer refuge in Switzerland.

In Switzerland, the family was welcomed by some of Zita's relatives. The Habsburgs felt somewhat at peace for the first time in years. Each day, they attended Mass and Crown Prince Otto often served at the altar. They had plenty of family time, and even welcomed their sixth and seventh children during these exiled years. But Karl could not relax. Even having lost control of Austria, Karl was still technically King of Hungary, and he was deeply concerned about the events unfolding in that country.

Karl had left a proxy, Miklos Horthy, in his place in Hungary, but he always intended to return when the situation calmed down. Unfortunately, Horthy did not intend to return the kingship to Karl. Twice in 1921, Karl made bids to reclaim his throne. Horthy refused to step aside, and ordered that Karl be sent into exile on the island of Madeira, off the coast of Portugal. This was the end of the line for Karl as a ruler. Cardinal János Csernoch, Primate of Hungary, visited Karl before his forced exile, expecting to find a "broken, fearful, suffering king." Instead, he described Karl as "fully and clearly in charge of his position," still keeping his "trust and his hope" through it all.[18]

Fully Exiled

Karl and Zita were forced into exile in November 1921. The journey was delayed because Croatian boat pilots refused to dishonor their monarchs by taking part in their exiling; a Serbian pilot had to be found instead. Along the way to the boat, the people of the empire fell to their knees and even wept before Karl and Zita.[19] The imperial couple had nothing but the clothes on their backs and did not know where they were going or if they would even be allowed to see their seven young children again. It was unclear who would pay the couple's hotel and food bills, or who would deliver the pregnant Zita's eighth child.

On a lonely Christmas Eve, Karl managed to send his children a telegram with a message of hope: "At Midnight Mass, before the Eucharist, nothing can separate us."[20] The Habsburg family was finally reunited in person in early 1922. The children's joy was "indescribable."[21] The family fell into a routine for what would sadly be their last few months with Karl.

Because of their lack of funds, Karl accepted an offer to move into an old summer house up in the mountains of Funchal for no charge. While this home had many elegant rooms and beautiful views, it was never intended to provide shelter from the bitter cold of winter. A chambermaid for the family wrote that "you could see everyone's frosty breath" inside the house.[22] There was also little furniture, thick fungi on the walls, and not always enough to eat. Still, Karl and Zita "refused to complain." They welcomed a priest to join their household, went for long family walks, and spent time in prayer.

Karl's Sacrifice of Self

During these months, Zita could see that Karl was making a "rapid ascent" in his spirituality, but even she did not know the details.[23] Bit by bit, Karl revealed to his wife that he had felt a calling from God since they were first exiled. God was asking Karl to give his life for the struggling people of his empire, so that they may once again experience unity and peace. Karl struggled with this deeply: He wanted to say yes to God, but the thought of leaving Zita and their children alone was almost more than he could bear. Zita could hardly find words to respond when he finally told her, "I shall do so!"[24] From there, his illness came on quickly.

Karl had always had a weaker constitution and lung issues, and in this damp climate he caught a severe cold that developed into fatal pneumonia. Karl bore his illness with a "profound trust in God." Zita sometimes wished he would rescind his promise to give his life, because she knew God would restore his health. Still, she attended her husband constantly, secretly watching him through half-shut eyes when he begged her to get some sleep. During several weeks of intense pain and difficulty breathing, Karl remained committed to observing the Mass from his bed and yearned to receive the Sacraments — Eucharist daily, Confession almost weekly, and, finally, the Last Rites.

Though he was only 34, Karl was clearly on his deathbed by the early spring of 1922. He exhibited heroic virtue in his final moments, forgiving all his enemies, especially the freemasons. Shortly before his death, Karl promised his wife, "We will always be together in the Sacred Heart of Jesus." His last words to her were simple and sweet: "I love you endlessly." Finally, Zita held a crucifix out for her weak husband to kiss.

On April 1, 1922, Karl died peacefully with the name of Jesus on his lips.[25]

Zita On Her Own

After Karl's courageous acceptance of his early death, it was Zita's turn to be brave on her own. A month before her thirtieth birthday, and after less than 12 years of marriage, she found herself a widowed, exiled, and disgraced former empress, with seven young children and one still on the way. Somehow, Zita did not despair. She sought the aid of King Alfonso of Spain, who helped the Habsburgs make a home on the Basque coast. In May, Zita gave birth to her eighth child. She named the child after St. Elizabeth of Hungary, because the Hungarian throne still rightfully belonged to the Habsburgs.

As World War II erupted, Zita and the children lived briefly in Belgium until the Nazis invaded, at which point they fled to the United States. There, Zita and Otto campaigned for Austrian independence from Germany. From 1945 to 1947, Zita toured around America and Canada, raising funds for the war-torn homeland she was not even allowed to enter. Later in life, Zita focused her attention on a new cause: her husband's beatification.

Starting in the early 1960s, Zita lived a more secluded life in a Catholic retirement home in Zizers, Switzerland. Following her husband's example, she refused to abdicate their God-given throne throughout her life. In 1982, Zita was allowed on Austrian soil again for the first time in sixty years. She was "greeted by cheering crowds, songs and posies."[26] It must have been a surreal experience, a ceremony from another day and age.

Zita was a widow for 67 years, but she was still able to find joy in her family during these decades. While Karl died before even meeting his last child, Zita was blessed to become the matriarch of a vast family including over thirty grandchildren and sixty great-grandchildren. She was overjoyed to see many of her descendants enter religious life, or to follow her example of strong Christian marriage. One great-grandson, Archduke Johannes, claimed that Karl and Zita, his *Uhr Gross*

Mama, inspired him to become a religious brother. "[T]hey had dedicated their lives to the poor," he wrote. "Their holiness touched me."[27]

Karl and Zita's Legacy

Soon after his death, Karl was venerated locally by Catholic Austrians. Purported miracles were associated with his tomb in Madeira, the place of the family's exile. When the tomb was opened in 1972 his body was found to be incorrupt! He was declared a Blessed in 2004 and may be fully canonized soon. In the meantime, The Emperor Karl League of Prayer for Peace Among Nations continues to seek Karl's intercession and campaign for his cause.

At his beatification Mass, Pope John Paul II called Karl a "Christian statesman" who sought to follow God's will "in all things."[28] Karl worked for peace and championed the rights of ethnic minorities. Catholic social teaching came to life as it has almost nowhere else throughout history. Karl was a Christian first, and a king second.

Blessed Karl I's feast day is celebrated Oct. 21, the anniversary of his 1911 marriage to Zita. His faithful wife died on March 14, 1989 at the impressive age of 96, and she has now started on her own journey to sainthood as a Servant of God.

This holy couple stuck together through many changes, including financial turmoil. After Karl died, Zita continued to work towards their goals: to serve God through his people, to protect Austria and Hungary, and to get their children to Heaven.

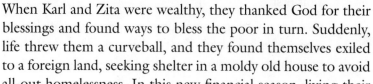

Marital Vow: For Richer, For Poorer

When Karl and Zita were wealthy, they thanked God for their blessings and found ways to bless the poor in turn. Suddenly, life threw them a curveball, and they found themselves exiled to a foreign land, seeking shelter in a moldy old house to avoid all-out homelessness. In this new financial season, living their vow to love "for richer or for poorer" looked very different. In both situations, though, they stuck together and tackled their issues as a team. You and your spouse can be a solid financial team, too! Learning how to appropriately communicate your feelings about finances and budgeting together to reduce the number of future financial disagreements are some good places to start.

Communicating Your Emotions

Upon their exile, Karl and Zita must have felt so many different emotions: fear, anger, shame, doubt. Even much smaller financial issues can cause us to feel similar emotions. The important thing to remember is that emotions are never morally wrong in and of themselves, but the way that we *express* them — or fail to express them — can be damaging to our marriages. For example, it's okay to feel frustrated that your wife has spent so much on takeout food, but it's not okay to yell and belittle. It's okay to be nervous that your husband will never find a better paying job, but it's not okay to hide these feelings from him completely. Being on the same team means that "her debt" is now equally "our debt," and "his income" is now "our income."

This may feel unfair sometimes, but other times it is comforting to know your spouse will stick by you no matter what life deals out. There's no quitting the team! So no matter how upset you feel or how large your financial concerns seem, remind your spouse you are committed to solving the issues together.

Some ways to share your feelings on financial issues appropriately:

- If you have big feelings about something, wait a day or two (if possible) to discuss them so you can calm down a bit first.

- Consider writing down some of your thoughts before a conversation about financial issues. These can help keep the conversation on track.

- Try this simple prayer before a financial/budgeting discussion with your spouse: "Lord, help me to express my feelings in a way that shows my husband/wife I am on their team. Be with us in this conversation and make it fruitful. Amen."

Budgeting

Budgeting together can help reduce future disagreements about finances. You will have to prioritize some expenditures over others, and this will likely be somewhat painful for both of you. It's normal to feel a sense of loss for your old lifestyle — talk about these feelings too!

If you feel doubtful that one or both of you will be able to stick to your budget, talk through a specific plan for keeping to it. Maybe one of you should do all the grocery shopping, because the other is too tempted to buy extra items. Maybe the other can look for ways to lower utility bills, like keeping lights turned off or not cranking the A/C quite so much in the summer. Both of you can pray for increased trust in God's plan during hard times. I have heard lots of stories about God coming through for friends just in the nick of time!

Some tips for budgeting together:

- Budget the way that makes sense to you as a couple, not someone else. Maybe you prefer to have everything written down in a spreadsheet. Maybe you prefer to set up automatic payments and savings withdrawals from your bank app.

- Each month, meet together and look over the proposed and actual budget for that past month. What worked? What might need to change?

- If you can, have some bigger trip or treat you two are saving up for. It may take months or years to reach your goal, but you'll look forward to it and appreciate it even more!

Riches in Heaven

In the end, you can't take it with you anyway, right? All the saints in Heaven are more richly blessed than the richest man here on earth. Saint John Chrysostom noted that even the emperor (probably the richest man of his day) would "throw himself" on the tomb of a martyr, pleading for the intercession of a saint who may have been a poor peasant during his life.[29] The saints have stored up riches in Heaven by their works on earth. We can, too!

Blessed Emperor Karl I and the Servant of God Empress Zita did not rejoice in their own high birth or wealth, but instead humbly sought to give all the glory to God and to serve His people on earth. They deeply loved their Lord, their homeland, and one another. When they suddenly found themselves exiled and nearly homeless, Karl and Zita remembered their vow to love one another for richer or for poorer. Through communication, humility, and thankfulness for the blessings they retained, they preserved their beautiful marriage.

The prayer below was written to promote Karl's cause for canonization. It pleads for the peace that Karl thirsted for his whole life.

PRAYER

O Lord Jesus Christ, the redemption You won for us gives
the world order and peace, which we too often refuse.
Mercifully receive our work and prayer
as an atonement for all injustices done against
Your Most Sacred Heart and against all religious
and earthly authority through rebellion and war.
May our prayers and sacrifices help bring peace to the world,
and atone for the multiple injustices, indignities,
and slander done against Your servant Karl of Austria,
and bring him soon to the honor of public
veneration as a saint. Amen.

— *"A prayer for peace from the Blessed Karl of Austria
Cause for Canonization."*[30]

QUESTIONS FOR DISCUSSION AND REFLECTION

1. What stood out to you about Karl and/or Zita? Which of their qualities or practices do you want to imitate?

2. What is one thing you learned from this chapter to help guide you and your spouse through future disagreements about finances?

3. What is working well with you and your spouse's budgeting system? What is not working as well?

4. How can you show your spouse you love them "for richer or for poorer" today?

CHAPTER 7

In Sickness and In Health:
SERVANTS OF GOD CYPRIEN
AND DAPHROSE RUGAMBA

FEAST DAY: NONE YET[1]

The vow to love our spouses "in sickness and in health" can cover many aspects of our marriage. It seems obvious that we must care for our spouse when they are sick or injured, but we can also look for ways to live this vow when we are both physically healthy. Other realms of wellness, such as spiritual, mental, and emotional health, as well as the health of our marriage itself can be considered too.

The Servants of God Cyprien and Daphrose Rugamba can guide us in living out many parts of this vow. When Cyprien was so ill he thought he would soon die, Daphrose cared for his physical body. Long before that, however, she had been praying for a cure for her husband's spiritual illness, which had made their marriage unhealthy too. In one dramatic experience, Cyprien was healed both physically and spiritually through his wife's intercessory prayer. After this, the health of their marriage was restored, and the couple spent the rest of their lives trying to heal some of the ills of their deeply wounded country, Rwanda.

Background and Education

Cyprien (*Sipiriyani*) Rugamba and Daphrose (*Daforoza*) Mukasanga were both born in the village of Cyanika in southern Rwanda, he in 1935 and she in 1944. While Cyprien's family was not particularly religious, Daphrose's father was a catechist, and headed a strongly Christian family. In fact, her father was the one who prepared the couple for Baptism when they requested it much later in life.

In 1954, Cyprien decided to attend the major seminary in Nyakibanda. According to his son Olivier, Cyprien "wanted to put God in his head, understand Him and grasp Him," and he felt that seminary would help him accomplish this goal. However, despite his studies, "God would escape him."[2] Meanwhile, his family was unsupportive of his choice to enter seminary; he was appalled at the scandals of some fellow seminarians; and he was distracted from Christianity by the writings of existential philosophers he was studying. Cyprien started to doubt the very existence of God. He left the seminary in 1959 and completely changed course.

Cyprien next chose to study history in nearby Burundi, and later in faraway Belgium. He found that he had a true talent for poetry, music, and choreography. He took a job as the director of the Rwandan National Institute for Scientific Studies and made a name for himself by working to preserve ancestral Rwandan art forms. In 1974, Cyprien opened The National Ballet of Rwanda, which put traditional Rwandan dance back on the stage and welcomed all Rwandans to join despite growing tensions between different ethnic groups.[3]

Meanwhile, Cyprien had become engaged to his great love, Xaverina Mukahigiro. He was truly devoted to her and was inspired to write beautiful romantic poetry about her. Sadly, Xaverina, who was a Tutsi, was killed along with several of her family members in early ethnic massacres in 1963. These massacres foreshadowed the horrific nationwide genocide of the Tutsi people that was coming. Cyprien was heartbroken, but because he still wanted to honor his commitment to Xaverina's family, he asked to marry her cousin. This cousin was Daphrose, a sweet schoolteacher who loved children. The couple was married in 1965.

Early Marriage

Cyprien and Daphrose did not have a happy start to their marriage. Cyprien was still haunted by his love for Xaverina, and the grief of an early miscarriage did not help their relationship. At their lowest moment, Cyprien packed up Daphrose's belongings and "returned her" to her family, which is a grave insult in Rwandan culture. After about eight months' separation and nearly a complete divorce, Cyprien took his wife back into his home, but their marriage continued to be fraught with difficulties. Cyprien had multiple extramarital affairs and even sired an illegitimate daughter.[4] Daphrose was most troubled, however, by her husband's disdain for her Catholic faith.

At some point in their early marriage, Cyprien changed from a questioning agnostic into a "fierce atheist."[5] When one of their children, Serge, was born, Daphrose put up a crucifix in the birthing room. Cyprien "grabbed it and broke it in two ... He just couldn't stand the sight of it," remembered their son Olivier.[6] Nevertheless, Daphrose never stopped praying for her husband and offering up all the suffering he caused her. With Cyprien's consent, she took all ten of their children (including Cyprien's illegitimate daughter, whom Daphrose lovingly adopted) to Mass each week.

Cyprien's Healing and Conversion

In 1982, Cyprien suddenly became gravely ill. The illness was very mysterious to his doctors: first Cyprien lost his appetite, then his sense of touch, and at times he even lost his hearing and sight. Daphrose cared for him tenderly and began to pray for his physical health while continuing to pray for his spiritual health, but Cyprien's condition worsened. At a loss, the couple flew to Belgium for new treatment options. But Cyprien was miraculously cured before he arrived! During the flight, he was suddenly "overrun ... by the Lord" in the midst of writing a song about his approaching death.[7] In his own words, Cyprien "started singing to Him ... and from that moment on, the Lord has never ceased to enlighten and attract me."[8]

In that moment, Cyprien was cured of all his mysterious physical symptoms but, more importantly, the spiritual illness caused by his hardness of heart also left him. He knew that he owed his physical and spiritual healing to his devoted wife's prayers on his behalf over the previous 17 years of their marriage. "After everything I did to her, she didn't leave me, even when I got sick. Instead, she took care of me," Cyprien said. "This is why her God will be my God."[9] Cyprien clothed himself in his newfound faith, transforming himself into a humble, joyful, welcoming man and a faithful, affectionate husband.

Happier Years

The remaining 12 years of the Rugambas's marriage (1982-1994) were "beautiful and joyful."[10] Daphrose was overjoyed at her husband's conversion and renewed faith in God, and Cyprien was constantly hugging his wife. Rwandans do not tend to show affection in public, but Cyprien insisted on holding Daphrose's hand, saying "I have to make up for lost time!"[11] He started helping with the housework for the first time. Cyprien's pet name for his wife was "*Marembo*," which means "gate;" he was saying that Daphrose was the gateway to their home and family. Annick Bescond, one of the couple's dearest friends, said, "I've rarely seen a couple ... so intimate, with such a complicity words can't express."[12]

While Daphrose had always taken their children to Mass, Cyprien now helped her establish a true Domestic Church in their home. They made one room of their home into a chapel with a tabernacle, and loved to dance while they praised Jesus there, often in the traditional Rwandan ballet styles Cyprien sponsored. The whole Rugamba family prayed together daily, and the couple made sure to teach their children love for the poor. Cyprien also took his family on a pilgrimage to Kibeho, a town in southwestern Rwanda where the Virgin Mary had recently appeared to several young women with an urgent appeal for repentance and conversion, warning about Rwanda's future if the hatred between ethnic Hutus and Tutsis continued.[13]

This ethnic hatred soon affected the Rugamba family directly. Cyprien was sidelined from his government job due to the increasing tension, so the family moved to the capital city of Kigali when he was offered a new job there. In Kigali, Daphrose opened a small stand in the local marketplace where she sold vegetables to earn a bit of extra money. When she caught hungry street children stealing her potatoes, her heart broke for them. According to their friend Jean-Luc Moens, Daphrose first befriended the children and taught them to pray the Our Father. But she wanted to do more.

Ministry to Street Children

Daphrose knew the street children needed love, stability, and support to grow into productive members of society. When she approached Cyprien with a desire to create such a place, he was enthusiastic about the idea. Ever since his conversion, Cyprien had been looking for new ways to help the poor.

In 1992, the Rugambas used their own money and some backing from their church community to start a rudimentary shelter. There they bathed the street children and washed their filthy clothing, fed them, and talked to them about Christ. Most of all, Cyprien and Daphrose made the children feel loved.[14] Unfortunately, the 1994 genocide halted the progress of their work. Since 1995, though, the *Centre Cyprien et Daphrose Rugamba* (CECYDAR) has expanded its reach through the support of Fidesco, the Catholic organization for international solidarity, and, more recently, Catholic Relief Services. By 2017, more than 1,300 children had been aided by the center.

Today, the CECYDAR takes in around 100 children at a time between ages six and 17. Often, the children have been separated from their families by war or orphaned by AIDS. They receive physical and psychological rehabilitation at the

center, as well as academic and spiritual formation. Older teen-
agers receive vocational training, and many can now provide
for themselves through farming or running a small bicycle taxi
business. However, especially for younger children, the goal
is always to reunite them with their own family or another
stable foster family as soon as possible. "CECYDAR is indeed
convinced," their website states, "a child's natural living envi-
ronment is always his family."[15]

The Emmanuel Community

During these same years, the Rugambas took on a second
project to help the people of Rwanda. While he was praying,
Cyprien heard a mysterious voice repeating the following
phrase three times: "I will, through you, by your life, accomplish a work of redemption." According to a friend, these
words were "etched in his heart."[16] The Rugambas believed
they could bring about this work of redemption in Rwanda
through The Emmanuel Community, an arm of the Catholic
Charismatic Movement.

In the summer of 1989, Cyprien and Daphrose were
invited on a short pilgrimage to *Paray-le-Monial*, a religious
commune in eastern France, where they learned more about
this charismatic community. All members vow to evange-
lize and serve God through whatever vocation He has given
them — marriage, singlehood, priesthood, or religious life.
They participate in morning prayer, Mass, and a daily Holy
Hour. They also value regular Confession, praying for one
another, and giving of their time, talent, and treasure as much
as possible. Emmanuel Community members meet frequently
in small groups called Households, which Cyprien and
Daphrose envisioned as one of the only places Rwandans of
different ethnic and social groups could gather in peace and
unity.[17] Cyprien told his community that what mattered was
not their ethnicity or political party, but that they belonged
to the "party of Jesus."[18]

At *Paray-le-Monial*, the Rugambas also met several dear
friends, including Annick Bescond and Basilissa Mukamasinzo,
and Jean-Luc Moens, to whom I owe a debt of gratitude for

giving me a first-hand account of this saintly couple. Jean-Luc would go on to visit the Rugambas several times, staying in their home and helping them start up their new chapter of the Emmanuel Community in Rwanda.

Daphrose, Cyprien, and their friends Annick and Basilissa made up the first unofficial Household. They began meeting in January 1990, and the Emmanuel Community of Rwanda formally launched in September 1990. Though the Rugambas knew their homeland desperately needed such a place of unity, they could not have guessed that war would break out in Rwanda the following month. As a symbol of ethnic unity, the community became a major target for those perpetuating the Tutsi genocide: almost a third of the community's members were killed. Still, the community continued to grow, "with renewed desire to live out the Gospel."[19]

By 1997, the Rwandan Emmanuel Community had 100 members; by 2017 there were 1,200.[20] Today, the community remains diverse, and leads local couples in a six-month marriage preparation class that the Rugambas helped create.[21] It is now the second largest Emmanuel Community in the world, after the original community in France.

"To me, it's like a fruit of the Rugamba martyrdom," Jean-Luc Moens told me. "The Community engaged in a unique work of forgiveness and pacification following Cyprien who had always proclaimed: 'There are no Hutus or Tutsis, there are only children of God!'"[22]

The Rwandan Civil War and Genocide

As a well-known poet, lyricist, and spokesperson for the arts in Rwanda, Cyprien had a fair amount of influence. "Everyone knew his songs," Jean-Luc told me, "which spoke of peace, forgiveness, reconciliation, love ... and the Lord."[23] Cyprien refused to stay silent about the danger posed by increasing ethnic tension and hatred in his country in the late 1980s and early 1990s. He personally advised Rwandan President Juvénal Habyarimana to stop the registration of ethnicity on identity cards, because this helped Hutus easily make lists of Tutsis. He also spoke out against popular radio broadcasts that glorified killings of Tutsis in Rwanda, and which a Harvard study found may have encouraged an additional 50,000 murders.[24]

Though Cyprien himself was ethnically a Hutu, Daphrose was a Tutsi, and their children were half-Tutsi. Moreover, Cyprien's voice was becoming inconvenient in the face of violence and hatred. He was repeatedly warned that his opinions would place him on a hit list. Still, he and Daphrose courageously stayed in Rwanda, faithful to their work with the street children and the Emmanuel Community even to death.[25]

On the night of April 6, 1994, President Juvénal Habyarimana's plane was shot down. The Rugambas spent the night in Adoration in the private chapel in their home. Early the next day, they called Jean-Luc in Belgium, asking him to pray for them. He called again an hour later and was told they could hear gunfire and rioting outside their home; when he called a second time, there was no answer. Cyprien and Daphrose had been killed on the very first day of the Rwandan genocide, along with six of their children: Serge, Emérita, Cyrinus Cyrdy, Dacy Aubin, Cyrdina Marie-Hélène, and Ginie Colombe. The youngest of the present children was only four or five years old. A cousin's visiting six-year-old daughter and a household servant also fell victim to the slaughter. Three Rugamba children had grown up and moved out of the home before the attack; the last of the ten, Cyrdard, miraculously survived and was later able to share the horrific details of his family's murder.

When the attackers arrived, Daphrose begged for the chance to pray one last time in front of the Blessed Sacrament. A soldier struck her with the butt of his rifle, breaking her collarbone. The soldiers also shot at the tabernacle and stomped on the consecrated Eucharistic Hosts inside. Then, the Rugambas were lined up in their garden in two rows and shot. In the following three months, an estimated 800,000 Tutsis and moderate Hutus were massacred, many hacked to death with machetes by their own neighbors.[26]

Cyprien and Daphrose's Legacy

Despite their tragic death, Cyprien and Daphrose Rugamba's legacy lives on today. Their son Dorcy continues his father's mission to expand the Rwandan arts as a writer and theatre director. The charitable work the Rugambas began with street children in Kigali has grown into the CECYDAR, which has served hundreds of children, often reuniting them with families. Finally, the Emmanuel Community is flourishing as a place of unity for all people, just as the couple had hoped when they brought it to Rwanda. They were truly "champions of the marginalized," as their son Olivier later wrote. [27]

Cyprien and Daphrose Rugamba also modelled living out the vow to love one another in sickness and in health. Daphrose cared for her husband physically during his short illness, but more importantly, she cared for him spiritually during many long, difficult years of their marriage by praying for him consistently. She never gave up hope that God could restore his faith and the health of their marriage, and her prayers were answered. Then, the Rugambas were able to work as a team to address some of what was ailing their beloved homeland of Rwanda.

In a September 1990 visit, Pope John Paul II told the gathered public that he wanted to canonize a Rwandan couple.[28] Many in the crowd thought of Cyprien and Daphrose right away, though they were still alive at the time. Since their death, people like Jean-Luc Moens have worked to have the family declared martyrs. "They died because they were witnesses of love," Moens told me. "If the Church declares martyrdom for this group, we will have the beatification of an entire family, parents and children. It would be a sign for our time, which needs the witness of family holiness."[29] The beatification cause for this beautiful couple was fittingly opened in September 2015, just after the Vatican Synod on the Family.

Marital Vow: In Sickness and In Health

When Cyprien was physically ill, Daphrose cared for him tenderly, as if he had never mistreated or betrayed her. She was already used to loving him in sickness, because he had been spiritually ill for most of their marriage. Daphrose shows us how we can pray for all aspects of our spouse's health: spiritual, physical, mental, and emotional. When Cyprien was cured, he and Daphrose thanked God for the blessing of health and used this period to bless others together. When our marriages, or our relationship with God need healing, we can also imitate Cyprien's reconciliation to his wife and to God.

Loving In Sickness

When my husband, Chris, was a baby, his mother was diagnosed with Stage IV breast cancer, and given a 2 percent chance of survival. She was away from home for months receiving experimental treatment. During this time, my in-laws' marriage obviously looked completely different than it had when she was healthy. They had to find new ways to express their love for one another and help one another stay strong and hopeful. Through my father-in-law's constant prayers, the intercession of St. Peregrine, patron saint of cancer patients, and some incredible medical work, my mother-in-law was healed. She, like Cyprien, was truly blessed with both a miraculous cure and a long-suffering spouse.

Emotional and mental health concerns are sometimes swept under the rug. However, they can be just as dangerous and just as taxing on a marriage as more "visible" illnesses. If you are experiencing any sort of mental illness, you need not only prayer but also professional help. If you won't do it for yourself, do it for your spouse. Do it for your marriage.

Hopefully, you and your spouse will not have too many serious health concerns to tackle. However, even days your spouse feels a little blue or has a cold can be opportunities for you to love him or her "in sickness." Be his or her servant! God can help you grow in virtue and bond with your spouse through these frustrating and humbling experiences. For me, taking care of Chris when he had a cold or pulled a muscle was great practice for taking care of young children — Hello, bodily fluids and temper tantrums!

Some ways to love your spouse in sickness:

- When one of you is sick, communicate your needs to the other so these needs can be met. Be your spouse's servant and give your spouse the opportunity to be your servant, too.

- Find a saint related to whatever illness or condition you/your spouse is facing and pray for that saint's intercession.

- When your spouse seems a little down in the dumps, brighten their day with a sweet note or their favorite treat.

Loving In Health

Finally, when you and your spouse are both healthy, thank God! Health is a great blessing in and of itself. Furthermore, illness often distracts our attention from other blessings in our lives, so take a moment to be grateful for it all.

You can also pray about ways you and your spouse might serve those who are not as healthy. Perhaps you could donate blood, volunteer with the Special Olympics, play board games with the residents at a nursing home, or help organize a fundraiser for an organization involved in medical research.

Some ways to love your spouse in health:

- Try this simple prayer: "Thank you God for blessing us with the gift of health. Please show us how we can use it to bless others in turn."

- Plan a long vacation, or even just a Saturday "staycation." Enjoy this time together!

- Check your church bulletin for opportunities to give of your time, talent, and treasure to help the injured and ill.

Healthy Relationships: Reconciliation

When things go awry, marriages need healing just like our bodies or minds. Conflict can threaten, interrupt, or even fully break the intimacy between spouses. A small conflict can grow and spiral out of control quickly, but it can also be stopped in its tracks by the equally humbling and difficult words, "I'm sorry," and "I forgive you." After his physical healing, Cyprien had a lot to apologize for in order to heal his broken marriage. Daphrose, in turn, had a lot to forgive. They both had to show heroic virtue to restore the health of their relationship and be reconciled to one another after so many years of hurt.

When we look more carefully at Jesus' miracles of physical healing, they often point to restoring broken relationships, too. In Mark 1:40-45, for example, a leper believed that if Jesus willed it, he could be made clean. "I do will it," Jesus told the man. "Be made clean" (Mk 1:40-45). The man was healed of his painful sores, but best of all, he could then rejoin the society that had pushed him away due to his illness. According to the *Catechism,* God wills even more that all His people would be "made clean" spiritually and be "reintegrated ... into the community of the People of God from which sin had alienated or even excluded them."[30]

When our marriage is not as healthy as it could be, I need to be reconciled to Chris through apology and forgiveness. Likewise, when I sin, I hurt my relationship with Jesus and I need the Sacrament of Reconciliation. God is always waiting eagerly to tell us "Be made clean!" and forgive us. Even if we have as much to confess as Cyprien did, or even more, God will forgive us every time, granting us the "pardon and peace" we desperately need through His priests, who forgive sins in His name.

Some ways to reconcile yourself to your spouse and to Jesus:

- Seek out the Sacrament of Reconciliation, then pray, "Jesus, by the grace of this Sacrament, bring me closer to You!"

- I've said it before, and I'll say it again: Be the first to say you're sorry.

- When you're having trouble forgiving your spouse, think about these words of the Our Father: "Forgive us our trespasses as we forgive those who trespass against us." Forgive so that you may be forgiven!

With God, All Things Are Possible

Rwanda itself was very sick in the 1980s and 1990s. Ethnic hatred of Hutus for Tutsis was threatening to tear the country apart. Nevertheless, Daphrose and Cyprien Rugamba believed that, with God, healing and reconciliation were always possible — they had seen it happen both in Cyprien's physical health and in their marriage. Today, the seeds sown by this holy couple have indeed sprouted and produced wonderful fruit for the street-children of Kigali, Catholics involved in the Emmanuel Community, and the larger Rwandan community seeking to rebuild their broken society on the stable base of brotherhood and love.

What follows is the official prayer for the beatification of Cyprien and Daphrose, along with their children who were killed with them. The beatification of a family all together would be a significant and unique event in Church history. How exciting that we can pray for this beatification together as a community, and maybe even see our prayers answered in our lifetimes.

The text of this prayer reveals many situations where the Rugambas's intercession might be especially efficacious: when we feel lukewarm in our love for God, when we experience marital strife, and when we struggle to forgive.

PRAYER

Holy Father,
We pray to you for the beatification of the
Servants of God Cyprien and Daphrose Rugamba
and the children who died with them.

Through their intercession, may we always have,
like them, a heart burning with love for you,
an unceasing zeal for adoration,
an active compassion for all those who suffer.

Help us to give ourselves unstintingly
to the service of the evangelization of families and the poor.
In communion with Cyprien and Daphrose Rugamba,
we entrust to you especially couples
who are experiencing marital difficulties
and people who find it difficult to forgive their enemies,
and we ask you to make us instruments of your peace.

In communion with the children who died with them,
we pray for all the little ones, especially children,
who are victims of abuse and violence.

Through the intercession of the servants of God,
we dare to ask you, according to your will,
for the grace of... (mention your intention here).

Lord, grant us the peace and grace that we ask of you in faith.
Amen.

— *"Prayer for the Beatification of Cyprien and Daphrose
Rugamba and Their Children Who Died with Them."*[31]

QUESTIONS FOR DISCUSSION AND REFLECTION

1. Did you find yourself relating more to Daphrose or to Cyprien in this chapter? Why?

2. What does it mean to you to love your spouse "in sickness and in health?" How did Cyprien and Daphrose Rugamba live out this vow?

3. How can you be your spouse's servant when they are experiencing any kind of illness or injury? How can you let them be your servant when you are ill or injured?

4. Do you generally find it more difficult to apologize or to forgive? Why?

5. What does it mean to be "reconciled" to your spouse? To Jesus?

CHAPTER 8

'Til Death Do Us Part:
SAINT MONICA

FEAST DAY: AUGUST 27

Some people think the Church *bars* people from divorce because it is judgmental or power-hungry, but the reality is that the Church is *metaphysically incapable* of dissolving what God has cemented. The only thing that can separate a validly married couple is death. We agreed to this right at the end of our vows: when one spouse dies, the contract is void.

I suppose I could end the chapter right here, having satisfactorily explained what we meant when we told our spouse we would love them "'til death do us part." However, there are a lot of other things that can tie into a discussion of death and Christian marriage. If getting our spouse to Heaven is our most important task, then, in a way, his or her death is the apex of our vocational paths. Also, while the secular world might fear or lament death, Christians have a radically different perspective. Anchored in the hope of Christ, we joyfully await our birth into eternal life and the end of all the pain and suffering of this world.

Saint Monica did not have the holiest spouse or the happiest marriage, but she devoted herself to unceasing prayer on behalf of her husband, Patricius, and she finally won his conversion just before his death. Her prayers were also effective in converting her wayward son, Augustine. Not only that, but St. Augustine of Hippo is now honored as a Doctor of the Church and one of the most important Christian theologians of all time.

After Augustine found his way back to Christ, Monica told him that her life's work was accomplished, and she was more than ready to die. Monica did not fear death, but instead eagerly anticipated eternal life. She died soon after and is now in Heaven praying for us all in turn. Saint Monica demonstrates the amazing power of prayer, especially for our spouses and children, and she offers a wonderful example of the Christian perspective on death.

Birth and Childhood

Monica was born around the year 331 in the town of Tagaste, Numidia (modern day Souk-Ahras, Algeria). Christianity had rapidly expanded in Numidia during the few centuries before Monica's birth. Tertullian, the famous historian and philosopher, was born here at the end of the second century, and the first Numidian martyrs were decapitated in the year 180 for refusing to sacrifice to the gods. Many other martyrs followed in the years to come, including the well-known Sts. Perpetua and Felicity.

Little is known about Monica's family. Her mother's name may have been Faconda. Monica had siblings, but no one knows how many. What we do know is that she received a strong Catholic education, despite a schism in her local church.[1] Augustine thanked God that his mother was raised "in a Christian house, a good member of Thy Church, educated ... in Thy fear,"[2] because without her strong faith he himself would probably have been lost.

Monica's parents employed an "overbearing" servant woman who did not allow Monica and her siblings to eat or even drink water outside of their official mealtimes. Another servant once humiliated Monica when she caught the child sneaking sips of the wine she was supposed to be taking to her parents. These experiences, though painful, helped shape Monica into a person of virtue and self-mastery. A biographer described Monica as "serious, modest, obedient, gentle, full of attentiveness and concern for others"[3] from a young age.

Early Marriage

When she was about 20 years old, Monica married Patricius, the decurion (tax collector) of Tagaste. He was probably about ten years her senior. Though Patricius had a somewhat impressive job title, he was really just a "minor landholder barely able to survive."[4] He liked to pretend that he was richer than he really was. Patricius was a pagan, but he respected Monica's Christian faith, and might have even converted if he wouldn't have to change his lifestyle after Baptism. Though he was tenderhearted at times, Patricius was unfortunately "impetuous" and "carnal," and he was likely unfaithful to his wife.

Patricius was also known to have a fiery temper. Unfortunately, men often beat their wives at this time, so the local women were shocked that Monica never seemed to have bruises from her husband's "moments of uncontrollable rage."[5] Monica had learned to keep quiet when her husband was upset and approach him later with any points of disagreement when he was calm. She shared these secrets of peace with other women, and many benefited from them in turn. Though we rightly look back on the acceptance of spousal abuse with horror, it was a different time, and Monica had found a way to keep herself and others safe within the circumstances of her day.

Monica also played the peacemaker whenever she dealt with the gossip of the local women. When they vented frustrations about one another to Monica, she made it a point to never share any detail with the other women unless it would help create peace between them.[6]

Motherhood

Monica and Patricius had three children: Augustine, Navigius, and a daughter whose name is lost to history, but who is traditionally called "Perpetua." Patricius "expected his children to bring him glory and economic prosperity,"[7] and he was boastful about his eldest son's gifted mind. Patricius could not afford higher education for Augustine on his own, so he sought aid from his friend, Romanianus.

We know much less about Navigius and Perpetua than we do about Augustine. Navigius had a mild and peaceful temperament. He accompanied his mother and brother on the journey in Italy that we will discuss presently. Eventually, Navigius married and had three children. His two daughters entered religious life, and his son became the sub-deacon of Hippo. Perpetua also entered religious life after she was widowed. She became the superior of a monastery for women founded by her brother Augustine.

Patricius's Conversion and Death

While it seems Navigius and Perpetua had relatively smooth paths of faith, the path to conversion for Patricius and Augustine took years of prayer and tears from Monica. Monica's "greatest aspiration was to win her husband for Christ,"[8] and, by her example and prayer, she did finally gain his conversion just before he died. He requested Baptism while battling a fatal illness, and Monica was consoled at his death that he was in Heaven.

Monica and Patricius had been married for almost 20 years when death parted them. Monica vowed not to remarry, and instead began a "more sober and austere way of life."[9] She prayed twice a day at church and received the Eucharist daily. She also threw herself into achieving the conversion of her wayward son, Augustine.

Augustine: The Son of Monica's Tears

Aurelius Augustinus, better known as simply Augustine, was born on Nov. 13, 354. Monica had her eldest son on the catechumen list from a young age, but she wanted him to understand what he was undertaking before he was baptized and be ready to change his lifestyle.[10] Augustine considered Baptism during a severe childhood illness, but then recovered and changed his mind. He would not actually be baptized until he was 33. Later, as a bishop, Augustine actually preached against this custom of deferring Baptism.[11]

Augustine's eventual conversion was absolutely due to his devoted mother's constant prayers. Throughout his autobiography, he expresses how grateful he was for Monica's intercession. "I cannot express the affection she bare to me, and with how much more vehement anguish she was now in labour of me in the spirit, than at her childbearing in the flesh,"[12] he wrote. This labor of love began in earnest when Augustine went away for school.

Augustine did his secondary studies in rhetoric in Madaura and, later, in Carthage. The worldly culture in these cities negatively influenced him, and Augustine grew in sin fulness and laziness. Around age 18, he took a lover whom he never named in his writings, and together they had a son named Adeodatus. Two years later, around the year 374, he returned home to Tagaste. Monica would have welcomed him to live with her, but for one problem: during his school years, Augustine had become a Manichaean.

Manichaeists believe that no person can be held totally accountable for his or her sins, because humans are inherently a mixture of good and evil. This heresy against the Church appealed to Augustine, who believed in God but wanted to continue his sinful lifestyle.[13] Monica refused to live with a heretic, and so Augustine, his girlfriend, and his child went to live with his patron, Romanianus. Nearby, Monica wept and prayed nightly for her lost son, until God revealed to her in a dream that she would one day win Augustine's conversion. After this, she felt confident enough to welcome him back into her home, but it would still be about nine years until Augustine would stop "wallow[ing] in … the darkness of falsehood."[14]

Monica did not believe herself capable of convincing her well-educated, skeptical son of the Truth, so she sought out learned Christians to speak to him. She pleaded with the local bishop, Antigonus, and he gave her a message of hope: "It is not possible that the son of these tears should perish."[15] And so, Monica continued fighting for Augustine's conversion using "no other weapon than prayer" and her nightly tears.[16]

Augustine began to move around restlessly. His mother followed him everywhere, never giving up on his conversion. He first moved back to Carthage following a dear friend's death that deeply grieved him. Augustine became a professor of rhetoric, or what he called "tongue-science."[17] In 383, at age 29, Augustine snuck away to Rome without telling his mother where he was going. He taught there for two years but was not paid well. Augustine had no choice but to accept "more than basic hospitality"[18] from local Manichaeans, though he was already doubting the beliefs of the sect. Augustine was lucky to be sent to a better paying teaching job in Milan, where, after two years of separation, Monica finally tracked him down.

Monica and Augustine in Milan

Augustine "distrusted and despaired of ever finding truth"[19] at this point in his life, but in Milan he would finally find it. He was once again confronted daily with his mother's strong Christian faith, and she also introduced him to the eloquent bishop (now St.) Ambrose. Ambrose preached the Word with "such precision and depth, such zest and sweetness"[20] that he influenced the dubious Augustine. Bishop Ambrose played an important role in the strengthening of Monica's faith, too.

During this time, Ambrose was trying to stand his ground against another local heresy, Arianism. At one point the Arian civil authorities even sent in troops to take over Ambrose's church. Not willing to give up so easily, Ambrose locked himself away in the church with the faithful, including Monica, for all of Holy Week, 386. This lock up was a "magnificent experience of the living Church"[21] for Monica. She learned new songs and prayers and became more integrated with her new local Church community. Afterwards, Monica continued attending Mass nearly every day, and prayed at the church twice a day.

Around this same time, Augustine sent away the unnamed woman who was the mother of his son, Adeodatus, and had been his lover for some 14 years. Adeodatus remained with Augustine in Milan. Monica, who knew her son was incapable of celibacy, quickly found him a suitable bride, but it would take two years to arrange the marriage. Augustine was not willing to wait even that long, so "in the meantime he simply took another mistress to share his bed."

From the outside, it seemed that "the son of Monica's tears" was still far from conversion. But Augustine had totally left Manichaeism behind, had overcome his "skepticism, materialism, and naturalism," and was feeling frustrated with his inability to conquer his own passions and commit to conversion.[22]

Augustine's Conversion

In August 386, Augustine heard a child calling, *"Tolle lege!"* "Take and read!"[23] He opened the letters of St. Paul, which urged him to "put on the Lord Jesus Christ" (Rom 13:14) in order to overcome the desires of the flesh. "A light ... of serenity infused into my heart," Augustine wrote of this moment. He ran to tell his mother, and Monica "leap[ed] for joy, and triumpeth, and blessed Thee."[24] All her suffering and prayer had finally paid off. Augustine called off his engagement and gathered friends and family to a friend's villa, Cassiciacum, to prepare for Baptism.

From September 386 to March 387, Augustine studied and prepared spiritually for his Baptism along with his brother Navigius, his son Adeodatus, two cousins, two students from Milan, and a friend. The group was sponsored financially, once again, by Romanianus, but Monica also played an integral role. She was the only woman present during the retreat at Cassiciacum, and she "brought a much-needed touch of maternal affection and concern."[25]

Not only did she do most of the cooking and cleaning, but Monica shared much spiritual wisdom with the men. She taught them to read the Psalms, which were the "daily bread" of her prayer, and always worked to "transform all of their intellectual discussions into occasions of prayer."[26] Though she lacked the formal education most of the men had, Monica's strong prayer life and relationship with God had given her deep wisdom. Meanwhile, she was always eager to learn more, and loved to listen to the men's conversations.

Monica's Earthly Mission Fulfilled

April 24, 387 was likely the best night of Monica's life. At the Easter Vigil Mass that night, she watched her sons and grandson be baptized. At last, she felt she could die happy, and indeed had little desire to remain in the world any longer. "What I do here ... I know not, now that my hopes in this world are accomplished," she told Augustine.[27] In her last days, Monica thought more and more of Heaven, becoming "indifferent to the visible world."[28] In one particularly moving experience known as the Ecstasy at Ostia, she and Augustine were meditating together and felt that they actually touched Heaven — "that region of never-failing plenty, where Thou feedest Israel for ever with the food of truth."[29]

Five days later, Monica became seriously ill, possibly with malaria. She told Augustine that the fever would take her. "Lay ... this body any where; let not the care for that any way disquiet you," she instructed. "[T]his only I request, that you would remember me at the Lord's altar, wherever you be."[30] Monica died after nine days of illness in May 387, at the age of 56.

Monica's Legacy and Patronage

For a year or so after Monica's death, Augustine visited her tomb frequently. Then, he and his companions returned to Africa in 388. Augustine was ordained a priest in 391 and became Bishop of Hippo in 396. He finished his *Confessions* and also wrote *The City of God*, one of the most important works in all Christian history. As a Doctor of the Church, St.

Augustine's influence on the Church both during his life and today is enormous.

Monica's feast day is celebrated in the Eastern Church on May 4, the day before Augustine's conversion. In the Western Church, her feast day is Aug. 27, the day before Augustine's feast day. Either way, mother and son are celebrated together! It is no surprise that Monica's relics, located in the Basilica of Sant'Agostino in Rome, have been associated with the healing of many children brought by their mothers. There have also been miracles of restoration of sight to the blind attributed to St. Monica. Clearly, her earthly mission to spiritually heal her child and remove his blindness to the existence of God continues from Heaven.

Because of her varied earthly struggles, St. Monica is known as the patron saint of alcoholics, abuse victims, conversion, married women, patience, and mothers. The Association of Christian Mothers, a widespread community founded in 1850, relies on Monica's patronage and intercession as the members seek the conversion of their children and husbands who have gone astray. Her example provides hope for such people because she did "nothing miraculous or superhuman,"[31] but simply persevered in daily prayer.

Marital Vow: 'Til Death Do Us Part

As Monica prepared for death, she showed that she had her priorities straight. Having no one visit your grave was considered "the greatest misfortune imaginable"[32] in those days, yet Monica did not care where she was buried. She knew that what actually mattered was not that people visited her tomb, but that they prayed for her soul in Purgatory. She asked in particular that prayers be offered for her soul during the Sacrifice of the Mass, itself the highest form of Christian prayer.

In many ways, St. Monica spent her life preparing for death. She longed for eternal life with God for herself and her family, so she dedicated herself to putting them all on the path to Heaven. With Patricius and Augustine converted and baptized, and the assurance that her loved ones would pray for her soul, Monica was able to embrace death.

Loving our spouses "'til death do us part" will eventually mean caring for them in old age and helping them prepare spiritually and emotionally for death. If you are still young, you are still able to live out this vow by learning to embrace the Christian concept of death like St. Monica did. Because death does not part the Body of Christ, you can also incorporate some new types of prayer into your spiritual life: prayer for the Holy Souls in Purgatory, and prayer for the intercession of the saints in Heaven.

Grow Old with Me

Hopefully, you will grow old with your spouse. Caring for him or her in old age is a beautiful and challenging part of living out your final marital vow. The *Catechism* urges us to give the dying "attention and care to help them live their last moments in dignity and peace."[33] This can be extended to the last many months and years of life, too, especially for spouses who live all of those moments side by side. It's easy for me to "care for" my healthy, able-bodied husband, but what about 50 years from now? That's when the rubber meets the road. That's when I can really show Chris what I meant when I promised that I would love him in sickness and in health, 'til death do us part.

As we age, it is also imperative that we help our spouse prepare spiritually for death. Many people find a renewed zeal to build a relationship with Jesus and His Church during their "twilight years," and you and your spouse can encourage each other in this process. When the time comes, you may also be the one to ensure your spouse receives the Sacraments to prepare for death, like Anointing of the Sick, a final Confession, and a sharing in the Eucharist, as possible.

Ways to incorporate these ideas if you are still young:

- Get experience serving the aged right now by visiting an older relative or helping out at a nursing home.

- Encourage your spouse to grow in his or her relationship with Christ right now, and care for him or her during minor illnesses and injuries (see chapter 6 for more inspiration).

- At many churches, lay ministers take the Eucharist to those who cannot attend Mass due to infirmity or disability. If this ministry interests you, ask your priest about how you and/or your spouse could get involved.

Memento Mori

"Embrace" and "death" are two words you don't often see together in secular culture, but Christians have held this mindset from the beginning. While Romans and Jews feared anything involving death or corpses, the early Christians spent time praying in the catacombs, purposely built churches over the graves of martyrs, and sought out the relics (such as bones) of the saints. Even today, there is a relic of some saint or another within or under the altar of every Roman Catholic Church in the world. Death takes on a positive meaning to the Christian, as we have "already died with Christ sacramentally" in Baptism, and "physical death completes this" process of dying with Christ.[34] Sharing in His death, we can also share in His Resurrection to eternal life.

"*Memento mori*" has become a popular Christian refrain. It means, "Remember you must die." Remembering our death "lends urgency to our lives" because it reminds us we have "a limited time in which to bring our lives to fulfillment."[35] The idea is not to be sad this mortal life will end, but instead to prepare ourselves so that we can enjoy eternal life. It's about keeping the endgame in mind. Are you living as if you will one day die and face judgment? Is your spouse?

Some ways to remember your death:

- Reflect on the words we hear while receiving ashes on Ash Wednesday: "Remember you are dust, and to dust you shall return."

- Make a date to go to Confession (with your spouse, ideally!), then prepare for the Sacrament as though you were going to die immediately after your penance. How does that mindset change your preparation?

Praying for One Another In All Stages

There are three parts to the Mystical Body of Christ, the Church. The faithful on earth (that's us!) are called the Church Militant because we are constantly fighting for Christ against evil in the world. Those souls that are preparing for Heaven in Purgatory are called the Church Suffering, and they rely on the prayers of the Church Militant. Finally, the Church Triumphant — also known as the saints — have been reunited with God in Heaven. There, they continue to pray for the rest of the Body of Christ.

While you are both alive, you and your spouse should pray for one another daily. If your spouse dies before you, he or she will need your prayers while suffering in Purgatory. If you are the first to die, you may have the privilege of interceding for him or her from Heaven. No matter what, prayer for your spouse is vital! The Church Militant, Suffering, and Triumphant are all united together as the full Body of Christ, and while death may part spouses here on earth, it cannot keep us from praying for one another. So be like St. Monica and never stop praying for your spouse. When you are most frustrated with her or hurt by his behavior, when you most want to give up — that is probably the time he or she most needs your prayers!

- If you want to add more prayer for the Holy Souls in Purgatory, try this traditional Catholic prayer: "May the souls of the faithful departed, through the mercy of God, rest in peace." My family says this after the blessing at mealtime.

- Contact your parish to have a Mass offered for a loved one who has died.

- Pray for the intercession of a favorite saint to encourage you and your spouse on the path to Heaven. You could start with one of the prayers in this book!

- Ask God, "How can I put myself and my family on the path to Heaven today?"

May She Rest in Peace

In the "Ostia Ecstasy," Monica and Augustine experienced a small taste of the joy that was waiting for them after death, and Monica was never again content with the fleeting comforts of this world. As she peacefully died, Augustine was inspired to send her to God with these words, remembering Monica's earthly vocation to her only husband:

> May she rest then in peace with the husband before and after whom she had never any; whom she obeyed, with patience bringing forth fruit unto Thee, that she might win him also unto Thee.[36]

The "Prayer of Trust in God's Heavenly Promise" below is also attributed to St. Augustine. It is a beautiful example of the Christian perspective on death as the very door through which we can "enter ... in the joy of [the] Lord forever," a perspective that he and his holy mother St. Monica shared.

PRAYER

My God, let me know and love you,
so that I may find my happiness in you.
Since I cannot fully achieve this on earth, help me to improve
daily until I may do so to the full. Enable me to know you
ever more on earth, so that I may know you perfectly
in heaven. Enable me to love you ever more on earth,
so that I may love you perfectly in heaven. In that way my joy
may be great on earth, and perfect with you in heaven.
O God of truth, grant me the happiness of heaven so that my
joy may be full in accord with your promise. In the meantime
let my mind dwell on that happiness, my tongue speak of it,
my heart pine for it, my mouth pronounce it, my soul hunger
for it, my flesh thirst for it, and my entire being desire it until
I enter through death in the joy of my Lord forever. Amen.

— *"Prayer of Trust in God's Heavenly Promise,"*
attributed to St. Augustine.[37]

QUESTIONS FOR DISCUSSION AND REFLECTION

1. What does it mean to love your spouse "'til death do you part?" How can you live out this vow while you are young and healthy?

2. What parts of growing old and dying are frightening to you? Why do you think St. Monica and other saints were not afraid of death?

3. If you had a wayward spouse or child, how would you feel? How would you approach the situation? Which of St. Monica's actions might you imitate?

4. Have you ever prayed for the Souls in Purgatory? Have you ever prayed for the intercession of a saint in Heaven? How do you feel about these practices? How might you incorporate them into your prayer life?

CHAPTER 9

The Most Exemplary Marriage
of All Time:
SAINTS MARY AND JOSEPH

FEAST DAY: SUNDAY AFTER CHRISTMAS
(FEAST OF THE HOLY FAMILY)

In the Cathedral of San Lorenzo in Perugia, Italy, a simple ring hangs on display. Scores of engaged and married couples come to visit this ring on certain days each year. They touch their own rings to it and pray that they would be given superabundant grace to be better husbands and wives in imitation of the most exemplary marriage of all time. According to pious legend, this *"Santo Anello,"* or holy ring, is the ring that St. Joseph gave to the Blessed Virgin Mary at their betrothal.

While we would do well to imitate any of the married saints, "authentic devotion to Mary" and her husband, St. Joseph, "constitutes a special instrument for nourishing loving communion in the family"[1] because the Holy Family is the prototype for all Christian families. God entrusted His only Son to this family — I don't think we need any further proof of their credentials!

I wouldn't dream of leaving the Holy Family out of this book, and yet it feels wrong to ascribe only one marital vow to their chapter. So, this chapter will look different from the previous eight. After giving some background information about Our Lady and St. Joseph, I will refresh your memory about each of the eight Catholic marriage vows we have studied and place each one in the context of the Holy Family.

Lineage and Childhood of Mary

Sacred Tradition tells us more about Mary's family of origin than about her husband's. In fact, Mary's parents, Anne and Joachim, are both canonized saints. Because they are grandparents to Jesus Himself, Sts. Anne and Joachim are honored as the patron saints of grandparents. They share a feast day on July 26.

Stories about Anne, Joachim, and the young Virgin Mary appear in several extra-biblical sources including the Protoevangelium of James from the end of the second century.[2] These sources tell us that Joachim was originally from Galilee. As married adults, he and Anne lived near the city of Jerusalem. Like their relatives Elizabeth and Zechariah, Anne and Joachim carried the heavy cross of infertility for many years. Joachim was even turned away from donating charitably to the Temple because, as previously mentioned, his community saw his childlessness as a curse from God. After this, he withdrew to the desert for quite some time, to mourn and beg God to send him a child despite his advanced age.

In the desert, an angel visited Joachim and announced that God had heard his prayer. Anne, who had also received an angelic messenger, was overjoyed to have her husband back home and, at long last, to be expecting a baby. That baby was the Blessed Virgin Mary, and her Immaculate Conception occurred within Anne's womb. If Jesus was born in or close to the year 2 or 3 B.C., and Mary was 13 or 14 years old when He was born, we can date Mary's birth to about 15 or 16 B.C.[3]

Mary was set apart and kept from everything impure from birth. At age 3, Anne and Joachim brought her to serve at the Temple of the Lord. They noted that she never looked back, a sign of her great holiness. She spent the next nine years at that Temple praying, studying, knitting, and cleaning, until the priests arranged for her marriage at age 12.

Lineage and Childhood of Joseph

We do not know when Joseph was born, but he was most likely older than his wife. Indeed, many paintings and stories portray him as *much* older, but as Mother Angelica quipped, "old men don't walk to Egypt."[4] According to the private revelation of Ven. Mary Agreda, Joseph was 31 when Jesus was born.[5] If Joseph was indeed in the prime of his life at the time of Jesus' birth, we can place his birth around 50-30 B.C.

Joseph's lineage appears in two different Gospels, but while Luke calls Joseph's father Heli, Matthew tells us that it was Jacob. This difference can be attributed to the Jewish custom of marrying a brother's childless widow to father sons on his behalf. According to a second-century historian, Heli and Jacob were half-brothers. When Heli died childless, Jacob married his widow and fathered Joseph. Joseph would have thus been considered Heli's legal son, though Jacob was his biological father.[6] Tradition has not preserved Joseph's mother's name, and we know very little else about his life before he became betrothed to Mary. We can surmise, however, that Jacob trained Joseph in the trade he practiced throughout his life: carpentry.

So we know that Joseph was a humble carpenter from Nazareth. He was from the line of David, which is important because it legally places Jesus in the lineage of this king. Joseph is also described as "a righteous man" (Mt 1:19), which is a very high compliment signifying that he lived his life according to God's law in every way.

The Bible does not record one single word that Joseph ever said, which has led many Christians to think of him as

the "strong silent type." Saint André Bessette appreciated this
alleged quality of the saint. "When you invoke St. Joseph," he
said with a smile, "you don't have to speak much."[7]

The Marriage of Mary and Joseph

In those days, a Hebrew couple would draw up a marriage
contract and be "espoused," or legally married, in the first step
of marriage, called *kiddushin*. They would not begin to live
together until after the ceremonial wedding feast, which might
be a full year later. It was during this year of being legally married, but not yet living together, that the Gospels pick up the
story of Mary and Joseph.[8]

The story of the Annunciation, where the angel Gabriel
obtains Mary's consent to be the mother of Jesus, appears in the
Gospel of Luke. Next, in Matthew's Gospel, Joseph is reassured
in a dream that he should still take Mary as his wife, despite
the fact that she is pregnant, and the child is not his. We read
that Joseph wished to "divorce her quietly" because he was
"unwilling to expose her to shame" (Mt 1:19), but Fr. Donald
Calloway explains that this can be interpreted in several different ways. In his (and many other theologians') view, Joseph did
not suspect his holy wife of infidelity. Instead, he proposes that
Joseph knew that something so holy was happening to Mary
that he felt unworthy to be involved. Joseph's dream reassured
him that God had chosen him specifically to care for Mary and
her Child, and so he moved forward with the marriage.[9]

The little that we know about the rest of Mary and
Joseph's married days comes from Gospel stories that are
familiar and dear to many Christians. We will just list these stories quickly now, because most will be described in more detail
later in this chapter. Mary and Joseph went together to the city
of David (Bethlehem) to be counted in the census, because
Joseph was from the line of David. There, Mary gave birth to
Jesus in a stable because there was no room in the inn. They
were visited by shepherds and the Magi bearing gifts. Joseph
was warned in another dream that the jealous King Herod was
searching for Jesus, the newborn King of the Jews, to kill Him
(Mt 2:13). The family escaped into Egypt and stayed there

until Herod had died, possibly about seven years. Then, they returned to Nazareth. Jesus lived there, learning the Jewish faith and the trade of carpentry, until beginning His public ministry at about age 30.

Joseph appears only once more in the Gospels, when he and Mary lose Jesus on a pilgrimage to Jerusalem and find Him three days later, preaching in the Temple. Mary seems to be part of several stories throughout Jesus' ministry, though it can get confusing because there are many Marys in these stories! She was certainly there at the foot of the Cross, when Jesus entrusted her to the care of His Apostle, John (Jn 19:27). It seems, then, that Joseph had died before the Crucifixion, and likely before Jesus even began His public ministry.

The Eight Marital Vows in the Holy Family

It may not sound like a ton of information to draw upon, but we can learn quite a bit about the Holy Family from the Gospel accounts and Sacred Tradition. God would not have sent His Son to grow up observing an unstable marriage, so we can know with confidence that Mary and Joseph lived out all eight of the Catholic marital vows we have studied throughout this book. It's been a few pages since we started this journey, so let's recap each vow and then see where we can find it expressed in this most holy marriage.

Loving Freely

In chapter 1, we focused on our vow to love our spouses freely. We saw how fasting and self-denial could help us break attachments to material things, and that frequent reception of the Sacraments can free us from slavery to sin. The aim is to become masters of ourselves, so that we are free to truly give ourselves to our spouses in marriage.

If detachment from sin helps us to love more freely, the Virgin Mary was freer to love than any other human ever has been (besides her Son), because she was sinless. Sometimes I feel sorry for St. Joseph, being that he was the only member of the Holy Family to experience original sin (whether or not he actually succumbed to sin is not definitively taught). That had

to be humbling! But Joseph exemplifies the vow to love freely
in his own way too. He is Mary's "most chaste" spouse, and
"chastity is freedom from possessiveness." Joseph "knew how
to love with extraordinary freedom" because he always put
Mary and Jesus before himself.[10] This remained true through
the centuries as well, with Joseph content to stay quietly off to
the side, directing honor to his wife and their Son. We will talk
a bit more about that soon!

When they were individually approached by angels, Mary
freely chose to be the obedient handmaid of the Lord, and
Joseph freely chose to go through with marrying his pregnant
fiancée and becoming Jesus' foster dad. They were not choosing the easy path. Mary and Joseph may not have foreseen all
the danger and sorrow they would face as Jesus' parents, but
they certainly knew there would be some. Mary's pregnancy
alone would have made their family the subject of baseless
rumors, ridicule, and societal shame. Jesus' kingship and divinity were sure to cause tensions among the current religious
and political leadership. Despite all this, they each said "yes"
to God and to one another.

The Bible does not record Mary or Joseph's specific
mortifications, but they certainly would have participated in
traditional fasts throughout the Jewish calendar. Though they
lacked the Sacraments of the modern Church, we know that
the Holy Family also participated as fully as possible in the
liturgical traditions available to them. Mary observed ritual
cleansing after Jesus' birth, and Jesus Himself was presented
in the Temple for circumcision as was customary (Lk 2:22-
24). We know they made at least the one fateful pilgrimage to
Jerusalem too!

Loving Fully

Chapter 2 explores our vow to love our spouses fully. This
means loving your spouse with all his or her faults and trou-
bles, not despite them. It also means sharing the weight of
your spouse's burdens — and sometimes even carrying their
full weight when your spouse is unable to do so. Though it
might make life easier at times, we have vowed not to cut our-

selves free from our spouses when things get tough. We have hope that our spouses will be there in our darkest moments too. Finally, this second vow reminds us not to hold anything back from our spouses. If a husband does not give his full gift of self to his wife, how can she love him fully?

Mary loved God fully, so she gave the "undivided gift of herself to God's will" when she assented to be the Mother of Jesus.[11] At this point, Joseph also had to make a choice. Mary was now associated with scandal and shame (though it was unjustly attributed). Mary's premarital pregnancy would affect their marriage, their image in the eyes of the community, and probably even Joseph's carpentry business, as some customers would likely ditch him for a carpenter not associated with scandal. Joseph could have avoided all these complications by simply divorcing Mary, but he did not abandon her in her time of need. He loved her fully — difficulties, crosses, and all.

Because Mary was immaculately conceived, Joseph did not have to love his wife despite her sins. But Joseph probably did have such sins and faults, and all of us do too. In marriage, we learn to love one another with these sins and faults. At the same time, our marriages can also be the schools where we learn to cut sin out of our lives. "Getting married does not ... magically confer perfection," the U.S. Conference of Catholic Bishops (USCCB) reminds us. "Rather, the love to which the spouses have been configured is powerful enough to transform their whole life's journey so that it becomes a journey toward perfection."[12] Joseph may have had it a little easier than we do, guided by a spouse who was already perfect. Still, these words are encouraging to everyone seeking to move closer to perfection each day, hand in hand with our own imperfect spouses.

Loving Faithfully

In chapter 3, we learned that loving faithfully means so much more than avoiding extramarital affairs. A faithful husband prioritizes his wife, putting her first and reminding her that she matters most. Additionally, a faithful wife seeks to resolve any conflict as quickly as possible to preserve the precious intimacy she shares with her husband.

Calling Mary and Joseph the ultimate example of faithfulness may have seemed like a joke to some of their neighbors. Mary got pregnant before she ever lived with her husband, so outside observers assumed she had been unfaithful to him. The truth is that Mary was ever-faithful to both her husband and the Lord. Joseph, in turn, showed his faithfulness to Mary and her Son when he led them swiftly into Egypt for their protection. This showed that he prioritized his family's safety over his own desire to return to Nazareth and continue the relationships and carpentry business he had built up there.

Mary and Joseph also showed their faithfulness to God through their obedience to Him. In *Hail, Holy Queen,* Scott Hahn contrasts the Eve of Genesis with Mary, the "New Eve." He notes that "Ave" ("Hail;" as in "Ave Maria") is the reverse of the name Eva (Eve). Likewise, Mary reversed Eve's disobedience to God.[13] Whereas Eve ate the forbidden fruit and led Adam into the same sin, Mary was God's obedient handmaid and led others to obey Him. In John 2:5, for example, she gives a very simple instruction regarding her Son that we would all do well to follow: "Do whatever He tells you." The fact that this happened during a wedding feast reminds me to be particularly obedient to Jesus in the realm of my marriage.

The intimacy between St. Joseph and his holy wife seems especially precious. One day, the world would know about Mary's virginal motherhood and Jesus' divinity, but for many years, these wonderful mysteries were hidden within their home and family. To protect their marital intimacy, I am sure that Mary would have carefully "pondered things in her heart" before discussing any conflict with her husband. In turn, he would have responded with his characteristic gentleness and patience.

Loving Fruitfully

The fourth marital vow is to love our spouses fruitfully. Fruitful love does encompass parenthood, which may at times involve Natural Family Planning, adoption, fostering, or spiritual parenthood. However, there is more to this vow. We also discussed how cooperation with the grace of Confirmation can make the

Fruits of the Holy Spirit manifest in our marriages. Ultimately, we want the fruits of our marriage to become a bountiful harvest that we can offer back to God!

The Church teaches that Mary was a virgin perpetually — before, during, and after the birth of Jesus. This is reflected in Mary's question to the angel, "How can this be, since I have no relations with a man?" (Lk 1:34). She was already betrothed and would be moving in with her husband in a matter of months. If she were intending to consummate the marriage at that time, she would not be confused as to how the child might come to be!

While some speculate that Joseph was married before and remarried after he was widowed, there is also a tradition that Joseph himself was a virgin throughout his life. In any case, Joseph must have knowingly and freely agreed to have a non-sexual marriage with Mary before they were betrothed. God and Mary would certainly not have set out to deceive him.

So, instead of giving their fertility to one another, as spouses are generally called to do, Mary and Joseph each gave their chastity to one another to protect. We call this mutual guarding of virtue a "white" or "Josephite" marriage, and we have seen it twice already in this book — at the beginning of the Martins' marriage and the end of the Quattrocchis'. Their fruits may look different than most marriages, but Josephite marriages can still be very fruitful!

Despite their perfect chastity, Mary and Joseph did, of course, have a child. They were holy and upright parents to Jesus and have served as spiritual parents to millions. Christians who had poor relationships (or no relationship at all) with an earthly mother or father have especially found comfort in the spiritual parenthood Sts. Mary and Joseph offer to them.

Mary's offspring, according to Scott Hahn, are "all those who keep the commandments of God and bear testimony to Jesus."[14] We are members of the Body of Christ, and Mary is His mother, so she is also "clearly the mother of the members of Christ."[15] For his part, St. Joseph reminds us that fatherhood is not always biological, as he was an exemplary foster father to Jesus. As Pope Francis writes in his apostolic letter on

St. Joseph, *Patris Corde* (*A Father's Heart*), "A man does not become a father simply by bringing a child into the world, but by taking up the responsibility to care for that child."[16]

I can think of a host of prayers and songs that reflect on the abundant Fruits of the Holy Spirit visible in these saints and their marriage. We sing about Mary the "*gentle* woman, quiet light," while Joseph is revered in the Divine Praises as "her most *chaste* spouse." First and foremost, though, the Holy Family is overflowing with the fruit of *peace*. In 1958, St. Joseph appeared to Sr. Mary Ephrem, SP, and told her that "[t]he imitation of the Holy Family … is the way for all souls to that peace which comes from God alone and which none other can give."[17]

Loving for Better or for Worse

In chapter 5, we switched gears from the four F's of loving freely, fully, faithfully, and fruitfully. Here, we focused on the vow to love our spouse for better or for worse. We learned how differently and beautifully the Catholic Church views suffering during tough times. If we give God all the best and worst parts of our lives and marriages, we can trust that He will use and redeem them all in His perfect plan.

Tracing the highs and lows that the Holy Family experienced is truly a roller coaster ride! Mary experienced the greatest joy in bearing Jesus, but it is putting it lightly to say that her neighbors would have frowned on the situation. In fact, it would have been customary to have Mary stoned to death for being pregnant outside of wedlock. The Visitation to Elizabeth, which we reflected on at length, was a "for better" period, a time of peace and blessing. After she returned from this visit, the very pregnant Mary had to ride on a donkey (yikes!) and give birth in a dirty stable far from home. She and Joseph then welcomed the Christ Child and watched as angels sang His praises and Magi arrived from distant lands to do Him homage. But soon, the family was on the move once more, fleeing to Egypt so that Herod's men would not kill their newborn Baby. All of this occurred in just their first year or two of marriage!

There must have been so many unrecorded moments of joy and awe watching the Son of God grow up. But there were trials there too. Scripture tells us that, while returning from a pilgrimage to Jerusalem, Mary and Joseph lost Jesus for three days. As a mother myself, I have felt my heart hit the floor when I have lost one of my children. But I have only "lost" them for a minute or two, and none of my children are the Lord of the Universe! Can you imagine the anguish and guilt Mary and Joseph would have felt while Jesus was missing, or the overwhelming relief upon finding Him in the Temple?

Mary witnessed so many of the highs and lows of Jesus' public ministry, from encouraging Him to perform his first public miracle at the Wedding of Cana, to the absolute devastation of watching Him suffer and die on the Cross. As we have mentioned, Joseph had died before all of this, but that does not mean that he did not experience any suffering related to Jesus' Passion. Allow me to explain.

When Mary and Joseph brought Jesus to be presented in the Temple, the prophet Simeon foretold that a sword would pierce Mary's soul when people opposed her Son. He said nothing of the sort about Joseph, and so Fr. Calloway notes that Joseph likely understood that he would die before these things occurred. If this was the case, Joseph would have experienced great sorrow knowing that Mary and Jesus would have to suffer without him there to comfort them.[18] He understood why he needed to be out of the picture (more on this in a bit), but he also wanted to be there for his wife and Son in their darkest "for worse" moment of all.

All these experiences finally culminated in the Glorious Mysteries of Jesus' Resurrection and Ascension, and Mary's Assumption and Coronation as Queen of Heaven. Mary and Joseph's "for better" and "for worse" moments were more extreme than any we will experience, but we can certainly seek to imitate their virtue throughout all these seasons of their lives together.

Loving for Richer or for Poorer

Chapter 6 focused on the vow to love our spouse for richer or
for poorer. In this chapter, we explored some practical ways to
manage family finances together with our spouse and to share
the blessings God gives us with His people.

We do not know many details of the Holy Family's financial situation, but tradition tells us that St. Joseph was a carpenter. This was a "blue-collar" job, and the couple was likely
from the lower middle class. As I mentioned, Joseph's already
humble trade may have also been negatively impacted by the
misunderstood "scandal" of Mary's pregnancy. When he and
Mary arrived in Bethlehem for the census, there was no privileged place reserved for them; indeed, there was no room for
them left anywhere. Jesus was the King of the Universe, but
He was ironically born in a lowly stable. After His birth, Mary
presented herself in the Temple for purification. She was only
able to offer two turtledoves as a ritual sacrifice, further evi-
dencing the family's lack of wealth.

Fleeing Herod after Jesus' birth, the Holy Family had to
leave their homeland and live in exile in Egypt. This was certainly another financial curveball for them! They had a home
and possessions waiting for them in Nazareth, but nothing of
the sort in Egypt. Joseph would also have had to restart his
business from scratch, finding all new clients among a community that did not speak his language and was likely hostile to
Jews ever since their exodus from slavery in Egypt. They may
have stayed there as long as seven years before returning to
Nazareth and starting over yet again.[19]

The Holy Family was not rich, but they had plenty of love
to go around. We learn from them that "[t]o hold the Child
Jesus in our arms and in our hearts is worth more than all of
the money and possessions of the entire world."[20] I think back,
also, to the image of the wealthy emperor crying out for the
intercession of a saint who was a pauper in this world. To be
sure, more Christians, deeply poor all the way up to fabulously
wealthy, have cried out for spiritual aid from Sts. Mary and
Joseph than any other saints in Heaven.

Loving in Sickness and in Health

The vow in chapter 7 is to love our spouse in sickness and in health. You or your spouse will face illness at times, whether physical or spiritual. Sometimes, your marriage itself will need healing. Apologizing and forgiving one another, as well as seeking the healing of our relationship with God through Confession, are vital to the health of our marriages and our spiritual lives.

Apologizing to my husband when I'm at fault, and forgiving him when he is, can both be very humbling experiences. Imagine how much more humbling this had to be for St. Joseph. He had to do all the apologizing and none of the forgiving in that otherwise sinless family! Any "illness" in their relationship was on him, but I am sure he was always quick to protect the intimacy of his marital covenant by seeking Mary's forgiveness. Mary and Joseph also had to stand together against some societal ills. Joseph in particular "shines as a model of courage and fortitude"[21] in protecting his family from the disapproving glares of gossiping neighbors, or the fear and hatred of King Herod.

Scripture does not suggest that Mary or Joseph suffered from a great physical illness that we could discuss here. However, Mary and Jesus had to support Joseph through the process of dying. They must have done a pretty great job, because Joseph became the patron saint of a happy death! Most of all, Mary and Joseph's Son Jesus exemplifies this vow because He came to heal all the spiritual ills of the world. Saint Bernard phrases it this way:

> We all suffer from a three-fold sickness: we are easily misled, weak in action, and feeble in resistance. Consequently, the coming of the Lord is necessary, first to enlighten our blindness, second to succor our weakness, and third to shield our fragility.[22]

Loving 'til Death Do Us Part

In the previous chapter, we wrapped up the list of Catholic vows with a discussion on loving until death do us part. We saw how Christians can actually welcome death because it marks the start of our eternity spent with God. We talked about praying our spouse to Heaven, loving them in their old age and possibly through their own death, and death as the fulfillment of our vocation to holiness and sainthood. These are all important parts of this final vow.

After Joseph's apparently "happy" death, Mary spent her remaining years supporting her Son. Mary and Joseph's marital covenant ended when he died, but her own life work was not yet done. It was important that she was there for Jesus' Passion, "faithfully [persevering] in her union with her Son unto the cross" and "joining herself with his sacrifice in her mother's heart."[23] Mary was there at the foot of the Cross when Jesus gave her to the Beloved Disciple and to us, then destroyed our death with His own. She got to experience her Son's glorious Resurrection, which forever changed the Christian perspective on death.

Finally, Mary was able to participate in the formation of the early Church, joining in community and prayer with the apostles and other important women (Acts 1:13-14). After all of this, her mission on earth was finally complete and Mary embraced death. She must have been longing to reunite with her Son! The Church teaches that Mary was assumed body and soul into Heaven, as Jesus could not bear to let His mother's body experience decay. Jesus crowned Mary High Queen of Heaven, and now we sinners confidently call on His mother and ours to pray for us "now and at the hour of our death."

Our Lady and St. Joseph: Our Most Powerful Intercessors

Our Protestant brothers and sisters often express concern that we Catholics are overly devoted to the saints, and most especially to Mary. Does she really merit so much honor? Why do Catholics have so many prayers and feast days for the Blessed Virgin? And where does her husband, St. Joseph, fall in all of this?

Our Lady, Queen of Saints

Venerable Bishop Fulton Sheen had a simple response to anyone doubting Mary's importance: "Our Blessed Lord himself gave ten times as much of his life to her as he gave to his apostles."[24] No other human being has enjoyed a closer relationship with Jesus Christ than the woman who carried Him in her womb, nursed Him at her breast, and raised Him in her home. Like any good son, Jesus loved to do the things His mama asked of Him on earth. Why should that be different now that she sits at His right hand, reigning as Queen of Heaven? Mary is, as it were, the Queen Mother to Jesus, King of the Universe and from the line of David.

In the Old Testament, we can observe how this relationship played out. Though the Davidic kings held the superior role, they often deferred to the Queen Mother's suggestions. When Bathsheba approached her son Solomon, for example, Solomon told her, "Ask it, my mother, for I will not refuse you" (1 Kings 2:20). We can put our confidence in Mary's powerful intercession, knowing that she loves us as a mother and will always point us towards her Son.

The Church offers a rich treasury of prayers for Mary's intercession, from the *Memorare* to the "Hail, Holy Queen." One of the most tried and true Marian devotions is the Rosary, which means "garland of roses:" each prayer is another rose on the garland we will offer to our Blessed Mother at its completion.[25] When she visits Elizabeth in the first chapter of Luke that we studied in chapter 5, Mary foretells that "from now on will all ages call [her] blessed" (Lk 1:48). We fulfill this prophecy again and again (53 times per set of mysteries!) when we pray the Rosary, saying "Blessed are you among women..." Mary is the most blessed of all the saints and indeed the mother of the whole Communion of Saints. You can always take your requests to Mary, especially those related to being a godly wife and mother. She will bring your prayers to her beloved Son, who will not refuse her.

Catholics start the new year celebrating Mary, Mother of God on Jan. 1, and we keep the party going all year. There are feast days honoring Mary's Immaculate Conception, Nativity, glorious Assumption, Queenship, Immaculate Heart, and Most Holy Name. Then, there are the feast days of all the Marian apparitions, such as Our Lady of Guadalupe and Our Lady of Lourdes. The month of May is dedicated to Mary, and October to her Most Holy Rosary. We also honor Mary on Saturdays throughout the year. We can never tire of honoring Mary, Jesus' beloved mother and ours.

Saint Joseph, Patron of the Universal Church

Father Calloway boldly calls St. Joseph the most honorable of all the saints. He notes that Catholics rarely even call the Mother of God "St. Mary," but instead refer to her as "Our Lady" or "the Blessed Virgin." Mary is in her own special category above the saints, leaving St. Joseph in the highest place of honor among the saints.[26] However, it seems that Joseph has often been overlooked in the prayer and devotion of the Church. Why is that?

Father Calloway explains that Joseph, in his humility, has always stepped aside to direct all honor to Mary and Jesus. Joseph had to die before Jesus began His ministry, because it made references to "my Father" (God) less confusing to his audience.[27] His absence also paved the way for Mary to become mother to John, and all of us, on the Cross. Most of Jesus' followers probably never met or heard much about Joseph, which meant that the evangelists had little to record about him in the Gospels. With so little to go on, only a few Christians held a great devotion to the silent St. Joseph through the early centuries of the Church.

More recently, though, the Church at large has finally picked up on this devotion. "Now is the time of St. Joseph," Fr. Calloway asserts.[28] Saint Joseph was declared Patron of the Universal Church in 1870. He appeared with Mary at Knock, Ireland in 1879, as well as in Fatima, Portugal in 1917. In just the last century, St. Joseph has been added to the Divine Praises and all the Eucharistic prayers, and he has been given a second feast day, a Litany, and a magnificent Oratory in Montreal, Canada. Like his holy wife, St. Joseph also has a day (Wednesday) and a month (March) in his honor. Saint Joseph's traditional feast day is Mar. 19 (honored as a Solemnity), but we also celebrate the feast of St. Joseph the Worker (and with him, all laborers and the dignity of work) on May 1. There is also a feast that is not so well known but growing in popularity among married Catholics: Jan. 23, the Feast of the Holy Spouses, or the marriage of Mary and Joseph.

Saint Joseph is a strong intercessor for his spiritual children, especially for husbands and fathers hoping to imitate his virtue in these roles. Saint Joseph was head of the Holy Family, meaning, said St. Madeleine Sophie Barat, "[t]he two greatest personages who ever lived on this earth subjected themselves to him."[29] Just as Jesus continues to listen to and honor His Mother's requests, He also loves to fulfill the requests of His earthly father. You can ask St. Joseph for his intercession in your need, or, when words fail, sit with this silent saint and receive his fatherly love.

What Really Makes a Christian Marriage Exceptional?

According to modern society and media, if you want a great marriage, you must search high and low until you find "the one." If this person is truly your soulmate, you will supposedly have strong sexual chemistry with them, and your mutual feelings of romantic devotion will be so deep as to carry you through to "happily ever after." The union of Our Lady and St. Joseph, however, was likely an arranged marriage. It was not based on attraction or romantic feelings, and the Church teaches that the couple never had any sexual relationship at all. How, then, could this be the most exemplary Christian marriage of all time?

The simple answer is that a Christian marriage is not made exemplary by romance or sexual chemistry. An exemplary Christian marriage is one in which the spouses strive to live saintly lives, rely on God's grace, and commit wholeheartedly to their marital vows. Each day, exemplary spouses choose to love one another freely, fully, faithfully, and fruitfully; for better, for worse; for richer, for poorer; in sickness and in health; until death parts them. God chose Mary and Joseph to raise His Son and to serve as the model for all Christian marriages because He knew they would live out all these vows.

The following prayer is from the end of a papal exhortation on pastoral care for families, *Amoris Laetitia (The Joy of Love)*. This would be a great prayer to lift up when your family needs extra protection from the evils of society, or when you and your spouse seek to imitate the Holy Family better.

PRAYER

Jesus, Mary and Joseph,
in you we contemplate the splendor of true love;
to you we turn with trust.
Holy Family of Nazareth, grant that our families
too may be places of communion and prayer,
authentic schools of the Gospel and small domestic churches.
Holy Family of Nazareth, may families never again experience
violence, rejection, and division; may all who have been hurt
or scandalized find ready comfort and healing.
Holy Family of Nazareth, make us once more mindful
of the sacredness and inviolability of the family,
and its beauty in God's plan.
Jesus, Mary and Joseph, graciously hear our prayer. Amen.

— "Prayer to the Holy Family," from *Amoris Laetitia*.[30]

QUESTIONS FOR DISCUSSION AND REFLECTION

1. Which marriage vow(s) come to mind first when you think about the Holy Family? Why?

2. We know so little about St. Joseph. What do you imagine he was like? What kind of husband, father, laborer, or friend might he have been?

3. What can Mary teach us about being a Christian wife and mother?

4. What is one concrete way you can better imitate Our Lady or St. Joseph in your marriage today?

5. Saints Louis and Zélie were abstinent for the first year of their marriage, Bls. Luigi and Maria Quattrocchi chose to be abstinent in their later years, and, of course, Mary and Joseph were the model of the "Josephite marriage." What are your thoughts on this practice? How would this make it easier or more difficult to live out the vows to love, for example, fully and fruitfully?

Saint Rita of Cascia

Conclusion

When I started working on this book, I planned to write about married saints and the Catholic marriage vows. I had no intention of writing about "other" parts of our faith, like the Eucharist, Purgatory, the Fruits of the Holy Spirit, or the Catholic view of suffering. This wasn't meant to be the *Summa Theologica* — it would just be about Christian family life.

But the more I researched and read, the more I realized that Christianity *is* family life. The Bible tells the story of God inviting humanity into a covenant, or family bond, with Himself, time and time again. The Church is a family of brothers and sisters in Christ. Even God Himself is a family. Pope St. John Paul II wrote, "God in his deepest mystery is not a solitude, but a family, since he has in himself fatherhood, sonship and the essence of the family, which is love."[1] Family is not one individual aspect of the Christian life — it is the be-all and end-all of Christianity.

The Church's Gifts to Married People

Because family is at the absolute heart of the Christian faith, one of the most important tasks of the Church is to support families. Countless men and women are seeking Heaven via the vocation of marriage, and the Church offers us three gifts as we walk this beautiful but often difficult road. First, we are given a comprehensive list of marital vows to help map the terrain. Next, we have the married saints to serve as guides and encouragement along the way. Finally, the Church extends the sacramental grace that will help us continue on when we are weak.

FIRST GIFT: Our Marital Vows

I have been to several weddings with unique vows, often written by the bride and groom themselves. These can be sweet, but they are often vague ("*I promise to cherish you.*"), impossible to keep ("*I vow to always make you happy.*"), or just plain silly and irreverent to the monumental undertaking of marriage ("*I promise not to hog the covers.*"). When we hear the familiar vows of a Catholic wedding ceremony, though, we have confidence that all the meaningful aspects of marital love have been covered, and that the whole Church bears witness to exactly what the couple has promised one another.

The Church has truly given us a gift in our marriage vows. The "job description" for a spouse striving to have a holy union is provided to us so that we don't have to reinvent the wheel. If you want to be a better husband or wife today, find a new way to love your spouse freely, fully, faithfully, or fruitfully; for better, for worse; for richer, for poorer; in sickness and in health; or until death parts you. The bulleted action items in the vow section of each chapter are a great place to start!

SECOND GIFT: Married Saints

It can be inspiring and encouraging to find individuals within the diverse Communion of Saints that we connect with in specific ways. As husbands and wives, we can imitate the married saints, knowing that imitating them will ultimately mean imitating Jesus. All the saints share God's deepest desire: that we would all be together as a family in Heaven. The married saints offer their lives and marriages as examples for us, and they are ready and willing to pray for us on our own spiritual journeys.

The saints we have met in this book had more in common than just being married, and their commonalities are noteworthy if we want to live like them. These saints had daily prayer routines, studied Scripture, and participated in the liturgical practices of their day. They built strong sacramental lives because they thirsted for more grace. They knew that God's grace would empower them to grow in virtue and fortify their marriages. The desire to reach out to the poor, sick, and needy is deeply evident in all their lives. Additionally, they all took on voluntary sacrifices and mortifications. Smaller acts of self-denial gave the saints mastery over themselves and prepared them to be faithful to God when larger sacrifices were asked of them.

All these common practices resulted in a general aura of peace around each of our holy role-models. Though each of them faced trials, even as painful as the death of children or their own martyrdom, the constant faith of the married saints protected the peace of Christ they held in their hearts. If we adopt some of their habits, we, too, can hope to see this peace abide in our own hearts and homes.

THIRD GIFT: Marital Grace

Marriage is too hard for us to do well by our own power, but thankfully we can fall back on marital grace when the going gets tough. In the very Sacrament that made us husbands and wives, we received the graces that will help us become saints by this vocation. The specific graces communicated in the Sacrament of Holy Matrimony strengthen us "to love sacrificially, to bear wrongs, to forgive offenses, to be chaste, to welcome and educate children, and perhaps even to die in the service of one's family."[2]

Marital grace will supercharge us on our paths to sainthood. All we have to do is cooperate with this grace by removing barriers to its flow within our lives and marriages. This means frequenting Confession and cutting out unhealthy attachments to sin and material goods. Then, we can call on God to get us through tough times by means of the grace He bestowed upon us on our wedding day (try one of the short prayers sprinkled throughout this book!).

For His first public miracle, Jesus blessed the married couple at Cana with gallons upon gallons of the choicest wine. In the same way, He continues to offer superabundant grace to bless our marriages. As long as we keep it flowing, sacramental grace will never run out on us. The Holy Spirit is "the ever-available source of [our] love and the strength to renew [our] fidelity"[3] to our spouses until death do us part.

Impossible Marriages

Now that we are approaching the end of this journey together, I hope that most readers have found at least one saint or couple to whom they can relate. We have met holy role-models from all over the world and throughout history, with varied personalities and interests. Some of their marriages have been mostly happy, others had rough starts or deeply painful moments. In the end, though, it seems like all the difficult spouses repented and the couples worked out their differences. I know this is not the case for all my readers.

Some readers may not relate to any of the marriages in this book so far because they feel that they are truly facing an impossible marriage. If that's you, I want you to know that I am deeply sorry. I want you to know that God has not forgotten you, and He has set aside a role-model specifically for people in your circumstance, too. Her name is St. Rita, and she is the patroness of the impossible.

Saint Rita of Cascia

Rita Mancini was born in 1381 in Rocca-Porrena, Italy. Her parents, Antonio and Amata, were great peacemakers amid the prominent vendetta culture. Though Rita wanted to be a nun from the age of 12, she stayed at home to care for her parents, and then eventually married out of obedience to them. Unfortunately, her husband Paolo was "proud and haughty," with a fiery temper and many enemies. Paolo was a "relentless persecutor" to his gentle wife, but Rita responded with humility and patience. She found consolation in her two young sons, Giovanni and Paulo.[4]

After many years of Rita praying and weeping for him, Paolo repented and apologized. He even forgave all his former enemies, but in 1406 a group of them ambushed him and stabbed him to death. Rita was deeply grieved at the loss of her husband, as well as horrified to discover that her teenage sons were plotting a vendetta against their father's killers. Rita begged God to either change her sons' hearts or call them to Himself before they could commit the sin of murder. Her prayer was answered: they both died, possibly of plague, within a year.[5]

Though she was barely 30, Rita was now a childless widow. She hoped that she could finally enter the nearby convent at Cascia, but several factors complicated this process. The nuns were hesitant both to welcome a widow, which they had never done before, and to be associated with the former scandals of Rita's family.[6] Rejecting Rita's third application,

Mother Superior told Rita it was "impossible" that she would ever even be admitted as a servant at the convent. Months later, tradition tells us that Rita was miraculously transported into the locked cloister by her three favorite saints: St. John the Baptist, St. Augustine, and St. Nicholas of Tolentine. "Rita," they told her, "the impossible is overcome in your behalf."[7] After this miracle, the nuns at Cascia finally accepted Rita.

The impossible was overcome many more times in Rita's years as a nun. When the prioress ordered Rita to water a completely dead plant to teach her obedience, the plant suddenly sprang to life. Many "impossible" miracles are attributed to Rita's intercession, especially for the blind, mute, and deaf.[8] After meditating on the pain of Jesus' crown of thorns, Rita was granted a wound from one thorn on her forehead. This miraculous wound was present the rest of her life, except the few months it disappeared to allow her to join a pilgrimage to Rome. From her deathbed, Rita famously asked a cousin to bring her a rose in the dead of winter. Impossibly, one beautiful rose was found growing right where Rita had specified: in the garden of her childhood home. She died in 1457 at age 76.

Saint Rita was canonized in 1900, and the faithful have become very devoted to her as patroness of the impossible. It is no wonder she earned this title: She was born to parents who thought they could never bear children; attained the conversion of a seemingly impossible husband; and saved her sons from committing a damning sin. She entered the convent despite hearts and doors locked against her, and today this convent even bears her name. Her body continues miraculously incorrupt today, still bearing the mark of the thorn wound on the forehead.

Living Through an Impossible Marriage

If you are married to an impossible spouse, marriage can still be your path to Heaven. To be sure, it is a heavy cross to bear on the way there. But if you embrace the suffering of that cross and unite it with Jesus' suffering, you will one day join St. Rita and all our other heavenly friends. *(Note: The Church never wants people to physically stay in unsafe situations. Even*

*if you have no plans to legally separate or seek an annulment,
please keep yourself and/or your children safe from a potentially
dangerous spouse.)*

Place your impossible marriage in St. Rita's hands and
pour out your broken heart to her. She hears you.

Saint Rita's very patronage reminds us of two things: that
some causes are truly impossible for us humans, and that God
welcomes us to pray that He would make a way where there is
no way. As the angel told Mary regarding the pregnancy of her
much-older relative Elizabeth, "[N]othing will be impossible
for God" (Lk 1:37). If what you ask of God is in accordance
with His will, "impossible" is irrelevant. Even if this is not
God's will, your prayers are never wasted. He has plans to
bring you to Himself in Heaven despite and even through this
impossible marriage.

Marital Vows

Each of our journeys to becoming part of the Communion of
Saints in Heaven really began at Baptism. The word "saint"
simply means "holy one," and in Baptism we become holy
ones because Christ dwells in us and brings us into the family
of the Trinity. As we continue on the path of holiness, we pass
other sacramental milestones, like our first Communion, first
Confession, and Confirmation. Then, as adults, most Catholics take religious or marital vows.

In some respects, this is the point where different Christians' paths diverge, because vocations to the priesthood,
religious life, singlehood (both consecrated and otherwise), or
marriage look very different. However, when followed carefully, all these roads have the same destination — holiness, also
known as sainthood. As married people, we have taken specific
vows and been given specific graces to help us become saints
by means of this vocation. In fact, the word for holiness and
marriage is one and the same in Hebrew — *kiddushin*.[9] The
Sacrament of Holy Matrimony radically changed the people
we have met in this book, and, if you cooperate with its graces,
it can change you and your spouse, too.

God's Plan for Marriage

The USCCB affirms that "all who seek to find meaning in their marriage will do so when they are open to understanding the transcendent meaning of marriage according to God's plan."[10] That plan is revealed throughout the Bible, where marriage and marital language abound. In Genesis, God creates Adam and his wife, Eve (Gen 2:7-23). Eve is Adam's "helpmate," a word that, far from implying inferiority, is most often used in the Bible to describe God in His role as Israel's helper. Marriage is established right here in the first chapter of the Bible as a natural institution, filling the intrinsic desire of the human heart to love and be loved freely and fully.

Sadly, Adam and Eve damaged the covenant of family life God had perfectly designed for them when they ate the fruit of the forbidden tree (Gen 3:1-7). But God had a plan! In the fullness of time, He sent His only Son to be born into and raised in a human family with married parents. Jesus even performed His very first miracle at a wedding feast, turning water into wine (Jn 2:3-11). The *Catechism* points to this miracle as the moment when Jesus elevated marriage to a Sacrament, explaining that "thenceforth marriage will be an efficacious sign of Christ's presence."[11] Finally, when Jesus died and rose again, He created the New Covenant, inviting us into God's family through a covenant that man could never rupture.

Revealing Holier Matrimony

When Christ gave up His Body for us, the veil in the Temple was torn, both literally and figuratively. No longer was the holiest part of the Temple accessible only to the high priest — now, everyone is welcomed to approach Jesus Christ in the Eucharist, day in and day out. The Temple had been unveiled. Similarly, in the Jewish tradition, the "unveiling" of the bride was the high point of a week-long wedding feast. In both these circumstances, Scott Hahn explains, "that which is veiled is holy, to be unveiled only in covenant love."[12]

We usually call the final book of the Bible the Book of "Revelation," but a better translation of the Greek would be "unveiling." Are you sensing a pattern here? The Book of

Revelation frequently refers to the Kingdom of Heaven as the "wedding day of the Lamb" (Rev 19:7), when Christ is united with His bride, the Church. That's us!

From Genesis to Revelation, marital imagery truly book-ends salvation history. In the meantime, "[t]he ability of human couples to beget life is the path along which the history of salvation progresses."[13] This Sacrament to which we bear witness, this holy covenant we have formed with our spouses, is the fabric of Christianity.

The Foundation of Human Coexistence

My young children enjoy creating towers by stacking things as high as they can. Generally, they prefer any other building material over the actual blocks I bought them for this purpose. My daughter, Ellie, likes to pull all the cushions off both couches, then stack them up with every other pillow in the house. My son Jack, meanwhile, has been known to stick the prong of his fork into the straw of his sippy cup to form a taller fork-cup-hybrid. How tall the tower gets and how long it lasts depends on the form and stability of the base units my kids have chosen. Though my children still do not believe me, squishy pillows and bendy straws will not yield as stable a tower as Legos.

Society is the same way: it is only as solid as its base unit. The base unit of society, or, as Pope John Paul II put it, the "foundation of human coexistence,"[14] is the family. And the foundation of a strong family is a strong marriage. Adults in stable, loving marriages are statistically harder workers, safer drivers, and more physically healthy.[15] This is because they know people they love count on them and watch what they do. In turn, children who grow up observing healthy marriages enter society better able to trust others, resolve conflict, and empathize. All these traits can work together to create a stable, peaceful society where everyone has a safe place to belong. On the other hand, rampant divorce, fatherlessness, cohabitation, open relationships, and infidelity have made the tower of our own society very shaky.

Pope Francis warned that "the weakening of the family ... poses a threat to the mature growth of individuals, the cultivation of community values, and the moral progress of cities and countries."[16] But, reversing this, we can see that *strengthening* families will protect the well-being of our whole society. Our marriages can form a level, sturdy foundation on which human society can grow and develop.

I firmly believe that saving the world can be as simple as going home and living out *holier* matrimony with your spouse.

PRAYER

God our Father,
We give you thanks for the gift of marriage:
the bond of life and love, and the font of the family.
The love of husband and wife enriches your Church
with children, fills the world with a multitude of spiritual
fruitfulness and service, and is the sign of the love
of your Son, Jesus Christ, for his Church.
The grace of Jesus flowed forth at Cana at the
request of the Blessed Mother. May your Son,
through the intercession of Mary, pour out upon us
a new measure of the Gifts of the Holy Spirit
as we join with all people of good will
to promote and protect the unique beauty of marriage.
May your Holy Spirit enlighten our society
to treasure the heroic love of husband and wife,
and guide our leaders to sustain and protect
the singular place of mothers and fathers
in the lives of their children.
Father, we ask that our prayers be joined
to those of the Virgin Mary,
that your Word may transform our service
so as to safeguard the incomparable splendor of marriage.
We ask all these things through Christ our Lord,
Amen.

— *"Prayer in Defense of Marriage,"* USCCB[17]

QUESTIONS FOR DISCUSSION AND REFLECTION

1. What is one of your biggest takeaways from this book? How will that affect the way you live out your marriage?

2. If you had to choose a saint from this book to be the patron of your marriage, who would it be and why? Alternatively, is there another saint not featured in this book that might fill that role? How might you incorporate your marriage's patron saint(s) into your daily life?

3. How would you define the word "covenant"? How does your understanding of this word impact the way you see your spouse and your marriage?

4. What is "grace"? What do you feel blocks the "flow" of grace in your own life? What can you do to better facilitate the flow of grace in your marriage?

5. In your opinion, what are the biggest contributors to the failures of modern marriages? How can you safeguard your marriage against these factors?

Recommended Further Reading

If you are interested in meeting even more married saints, I recommend Ferdinand Holböck's collection of short biographies, *Married Saints and Blesseds Through the Centuries*.

This book does not attempt to delve too deeply into Catholic apologetics. *The Catechism of the Catholic Church* is the best place to start if you want to learn more about Sacraments and sacramental grace.

Hail, Holy Queen by Scott Hahn expounds on Marian doctrines I briefly mention, like the Assumption and perpetual virginity of Mary. Another of Hahn's books, *First Comes Love*, is a wealth of information related to God being a family and the nature of covenantal bonds.

If you want to learn more about Mary's most chaste spouse, check out *Consecration to St. Joseph* by Fr. Donald Calloway, MIC. I would especially recommend this work to all the husbands and fathers out there!

To better contrast the Catholic view of marriage with Protestant and other views, I recommend *The Catholic Church Saved My Marriage* by Dr. David Anders.

Studying Pope St. Paul VI's papal encyclical *Humanae vitae*, as well as *Theology of the Body Explained* by Christopher West, will help all Christians appreciate the beauty of God's plan for human sexuality and marital sex.

For practical resources to learn Natural Family Planning, I highly recommend Whole Mission, an outreach of Marquette University, as well as the Pope Paul VI Institute, which is associated with FertilityCare and NaPro Technology. Catholic Women and Couples NFP, found at ccnfp.org, teaches NFP to Catholics free of charge. Various NFP-related Facebook groups and other online communities are also available to help you find a method, instructor and/or healthcare provider that works best for you and your family!

For more practical ways to live out your marital vows, check out the devotional *Forever* by Bobby and Jackie Angel. My own blog also offers tidbits to encourage you in your vocation including challenges to take on, Church teaching, more on holy role-models, and interviews with modern Catholic couples just like you. Check it out at www.HolierMatrimony.com!

Bibliography

Anders, David. *The Catholic Church Saved My Marriage: Discovering Hidden Grace in the Sacrament of Matrimony.* Irondale, AL: EWTN Publishing, Inc., 2018.

Angel, Jackie F., and Angel, Bobby. *Forever: A Catholic Devotional for Your Marriage.* Boston: Pauline Books and Media, 2017.

Calloway, Fr. Donald, MIC. *Consecration to St. Joseph: The Wonders of Our Spiritual Father.* Stockbridge, MA: Marian Press, 2020.

Donaghy, Rev. Thomas J. *Lives of the Saints II.* Towota, NJ: Catholic Book Publishing Corp., 2006.

Francis, Pope. *Amoris Laetitia.* Erlanger, KY: The Dynamic Catholic Institute, 2015.

Hahn, Scott. *First Comes Love: Finding Your Family in the Church and the Trinity.* New York: Doubleday, 2002.

—— *Hail, Holy Queen: The Mother of God in the Word of God.* New York: Doubleday, 2001.

—— *Signs of Life: 20 Catholic Customs and their Biblical Roots.* 2nd ed. New York: Image, 2018.

Holböck, Ferdinand. *Married Saints and Blesseds Through the Centuries.* 2nd ed. San Francisco: Ignatius, 2002.

Hume, Cardinal Basil, OSB, ed. *Butler's Lives of the Saints: Concise Edition.* 4th ed. San Francisco: Harper and Row Publishers, 1985.

Hunter-Kilmer, Meg. "10 Married Couples Who Have Been Canonized or Are on Their Way." Aleteia. Last modified Feb. 15, 2020. https://aleteia.org/2020/02/15/10-married-couples-who-have-been-canonized-or-are-on-their-way.

International Commission on English in the Liturgy. *The Order of Celebrating Matrimony.* 2nd ed. Totowa, NJ: Catholic Book Publishing Corp., 2016.

Kraft, Sara, and Justin Kraft. "Married Saints That Bear Witness to the Faith." The Mystical Humanity of Christ Publishing.

Last modified May 22, 2018. www.coraevans.com/blog/article/married-saints-that-bear-witness-to-the-faith.

John Paul II, Pope. *Familiaris Consortio*. Boston: St. Paul Books and Media, 1982.

——*The Theology of the Body: Human Love in the Divine Plan.* 2nd ed. Boston: Pauline Books and Media, 1997.

Landry, Fr. Roger J. "Free, Full, Faithful, Fruitful Love." Catholic Preaching. Last modified June 30, 2018. http://catholicpreaching.com/wp/wp-content/uploads/2018/07/Free-Full-Faithful-Fruitful-Love.pdf.

Paul VI, Pope. *Humanae Vitae*. San Francisco: Ignatius Press, 1998.

Roman Catholic Church. *Catechism of the Catholic Church*. 3rd ed. New York: Image, 1995. Also www.usccb.org/sites/default/files/flipbooks/catechism.

United States Conference of Catholic Bishops. *Marriage: Love and Life in the Divine Plan*. Washington, DC: USCCB Publishing, 2009.

Wojtyła, Karol. *Love and Responsibility*. 2nd ed. San Francisco: Ignatius Press, 1993.

Acknowledgements

I am deeply grateful to all the men and women who helped make this book happen. I learned so much from people who know more about the holy role-models in this book (or even knew them personally!), including Suzanne Pearson of the Emperor Karl League of Prayer, Maureen O'Riordan of LouisAndZelieMartin.org, Tracy Kinealy, and especially Jean-Luc Moens of the Emmanuel Community.

Thank you also to my "Book Mama," Kelly Guest, and to the Catholic Writers Guild's Nonfiction Critique Group. Your feedback and encouragement mean the world to me. Michelle Buckman served as editor extraordinaire.

Finally, the biggest thank you goes to my parents, Stasia and Patrick Rhoads. I am grateful that you read draft after draft of each chapter of this book, but I am so much more grateful for your steadfast example of holy matrimony throughout my life. I love you both!

About the Author

Caitrin Bennett is a homeschooling Catholic mama who truly believes that holy marriages can restabilize our society. She currently lives in Maryland with her husband, Chris, and their three young children.

Caitrin blogs at HolierMatrimony. com and serves as a monthly contributor at CatholicMom.com.

Holier Matrimony is her first book.

Notes

The Catholic Wedding Vows

1 "The Order of Celebrating Matrimony," the Committee on Divine Worship, United States Conference of Catholic Bishops, 2016. See saintdominics.org/resources/attachments/202/mass_outline.pdf.

Preface

1 See "Provisional number of marriages and marriage rate: United States, 2000-2020," *Center for Disease Control.*

2 Yeris Mayol-Garcia, Benjamin Gurrentz, and Rose M. Kreider, *Number, Timing, and Duration of Marriages and Divorces: 2016,* U. S. Census Bureau (April 2021), 1. www.census.gov/content/dam/Census/library/publications/2021/demo/p70-167.pdf.

Introduction

1 Joseph Pronechen, "The Step-by-Step Guide to How a Person Becomes a Canonized Saint," *National Catholic Register,* May 28, 2021. www.ncregister.com/blog/how-does-a-person-become-a-canonized-saint.

2 Father David Callum, "Married Saints," *Catholic Insight,* Feb. 3, 2016. https://catholicinsight.com/married-saints.

3 Dr. Jeff Mirus, "Married Saints?" *Catholic Culture,* Feb. 20, 2007. www.catholicculture.org/commentary/married-saints/?repos=6&subrepos=0&searchid=2292398

4 Scott Hahn, *Signs of Life: 20 Catholic Customs and their Biblical Roots* (New York: Image, 2018), 65.

5 Scott Hahn, *Hail, Holy Queen: The Mother of God in the Word of God* (New York: Doubleday, 2001), 26.

6 *Catechism of the Catholic Church* (www.usccb.org/sites/default/files/flipbooks/catechism), 1639. Hereafter *CCC.*

7 Ibid., 1616.

8 Ibid., 1624.

9 Pope John Paul II, *Familiaris Consortio,* Nov. 22, 1981, 11. www.vatican.va/content/john-paul-ii/en/apost_exhortations/documents/hf_jp-i_exh_19811122_familiaris-consortio.html.

Chapter 1: Loving Freely

[1] Hélène Mongin, *Sts. Louis and Zélie Martin: The Extraordinary Parents of St. Thérèse of Lisieux* (Paris: Editions de l'Emmanuel, 2008), 49

[2] Saint Thérèse of Lisieux, Letter to Abbot Bellière, July 26, 1897, as quoted in Mongin, 153.

[3] Mongin, 9, 15.

[4] Ibid., 16.

[5] Ibid., 15.

[6] Saint Thérèse of Lisieux, *Story of a Soul* (Washington, DC: Editions du Cerf and Desclée de Brouwer, 1972), 2.

[7] Mongin, 15.

[8] Ferdinand Holböck, *Married Saints and Blesseds Through the Centuries* (San Francisco: Ignatius Press, 2002), 404.

[9] Mongin, 17.

[10] Ibid., 19

[11] Office of the Postulator General of the Discalced Carmelites, "Biographical Profile of the Venerable Servants of God Louis Martin and Zélie Martin," Oct. 19, 2008. https://static1.1.sqspcdn.com/static/f/143555/2021306/1224046373503/BIOGRAPHICAL+PROFILE+OF+THE+VENERABLE+SERVANTS+OF+GOD.pdf

[12] Father Antonio Sicari, O.C.D., "Zélie and Louis Martin, Mother and Father of Saint Thérèse of the Child Jesus of the Holy Face," *Saints Louis and Zelie Martin, The Parents of Saint Thérèse of Lisieux* (2008). http://www.louisandzeliemartin.org/sicari.

[13] Office of the Postulator General of the Discalced Carmelites.

[14] Sicari.

[15] Mongin, 23.

[16] Sicari.

[17] Mongin, 20.

[18] Maureen O'Riordan, "Zelie Guerin Before Her Marriage," *Sts. Louis and Zelie Martin* (2021). www.louisandzeliemartin.org/part-2-zelie-guerin-before-her-marriage.

[19] Mongin, 55.

[20] Holböck, 408.

[21] Saint Thérèse of Lisieux, *Story of a Soul*, 21.

[22] Sicari.

[23] Saint Thérèse of Lisieux, *Story of a Soul*, 48.

[24] Mongin, 75.

[25] Ibid., 42-3.

[26] Ibid., 51.

[27] Ibid., 97-8.

[28] Ibid., 96-7.

[29] Ibid., 101.

[30] Saint Thérèse of Lisieux, *Story of a Soul*, 93.

[31] Mongin, 102.

[32] Ibid., 104.

[33] Albert H. Dolan, *God Made the Violet, Too: The Life of Léonie, Sister of St. Thérèse* (Chicago: Carmelite Press, 1948), 16.

[34] Mongin, p. 64

[35] Dolan, 35.

[36] Sicari.

[37] Mongin, 110.

[38] Sicari.

[39] Mongin, 125.

[40] Saint Thérèse of Lisieux, *Story of a Soul*, 33.

[41] Holböck, 409.

[42] Sicari.

[43] Saint Thérèse of Lisieux, *Story of a Soul*, 12-3, 104, 106.

[44] Father James Geoghegan, OCD, "The Parents of St. Thérèse," *Sts. Louis and Zélie Martin*. Last modified 2021. www.louisandzeliemartin.org/the-parents-of-st-therese-fr

[45] Saint Thérèse of Lisieux, *Story of a Soul*, 137.

[46] Holböck, 411.

[47] Sicari.

[48] Saint Thérèse of Lisieux, *Story of a Soul*, 16-17.

[49] Mongin, 7

[50] Saint Thérèse of Lisieux, *Story of a Soul*, 153.

[51] Pope Francis, *Amoris Laetitia*, March 19, 2016, 115. www.vatican.va/content/francesco/en/apost_exhortations/ documents/papa-francesco_esortazione-ap_20160319_amoris-laetitia.html

[52] Mongin, 407.

[53] Saint Thérèse of Lisieux, *Story of a Soul*, 4.

[54] Mongin, 44.

55 Saint Thérèse of Lisieux, *Story of a Soul*, 86.

56 Saint Augustine of Hippo, *The Confessions of St. Augustine* (New York: P. F. Collier and Son Co., 1909), 135.

57 Jackie F. Angel and Bobby Angel, *Forever: A Catholic Devotional for Your Marriage* (Boston: Pauline Books and Media, 2017), 49.

58 "Prayer to Saints Louis and Zélie Martin," trans. by Maureen O'Riordan. www.louisandzeliemartin.org/prayer-to-saints-louis-and-zelie-martin.

Chapter 2: Loving Fully

1 Monsignor Paul Guérin, "Blessed Mary of the Incarnation," Sanctoral. https://sanctoral.com/en/saints/blessed_mary_of_the_incarnation_carmelite.html.

2 Emily Bowles, *A Gracious Life, The Life of B. Acarie* (Oxford: Oxford University, 1879), 13-14.

3 Holböck, 350-1.

4 Bowles, 18-9.

5 Ibid., 23-5.

6 Ibid., 35-37.

7 Ibid., 48.

8 Ibid., 54-58.

9 Ibid., 24.

10 Rev. Thomas J. Donaghy, *Lives of the Saints II* (Totowa, NJ: Catholic Book Publishing Corp., 2006), 176.

11 Bowles, 108-9.

12 Ibid., 66.

13 Ibid., 26-7.

14 Ibid., 27-9.

15 Ibid., 32-33.

16 See Discalced Carmelites of the Australia-Oceania Region: https://carmelite.com/kc-section/spirituality-backup/

17 Donaghy, 176.

18 Bowles, 50.

19 Ibid., 230.

20 Holböck, 352.

21 Karol Wojtyła, *Love and Responsibility* (San Francisco: Ignatius Press, 1993), 239; emphasis mine.

22 Pope St. Paul VI, *Humanae vitae*, July 26, 1968, 12; emphasis

mine. www.vatican.va/content/paul-vi/en/encyclicals/documents/hf_p-vi_enc_25071968_humanae-vitae.html.

23 See Fr. Roger J. Landry, "Free, Full, Faithful, Fruitful Love," *Catholic Preaching*, June 30, 2018. http://catholicpreaching.com/wp/wp-content/uploads/2018/07/Free-Full-Faithful-Fruitful-Love.pdf.

24 Saint Francis de Sales, "Act of Abandonment," *Catholic Online*. www.catholic.org/prayers/prayer.php?p=518.

Chapter 3: Loving Faithfully

1 Peter Ackroyd, *The Life of Thomas More* (New York: Anchor Books, 1999), 9.

2 Ibid., 63.

3 Ibid., 55, 56.

4 Ibid., 296-7.

5 Ibid., 119.

6 Ibid., 142.

7 Holböck, 323.

8 Father Thomas J. McGovern, "Family, Friendship and Divine Filiation: St. Thomas More 1478-1535," *Christendom Awake*, Feb. 12, 2003. http://christendom-awake.org/pages/mcgovern/tmfamily.htm.

9 Ackroyd, 259.

10 McGovern.

11 Ackroyd, 83.

12 Susan Abernathy, "Margaret Roper, Daughter of Sir Thomas More," *The Freelance History Writer*, July 19, 2012. https://thefreelancehistorywriter.com/2012/07/19/margaret-roper-daughter-of-sir-thomas-more.

13 Desiderius Erasmus, "Final Comments About Thomas More by Erasmus," *Thomas More Studies*, 2023. https://thomasmorestudies.org/wp-content/uploads/2020/08/ErasmusFinalComments1535.pdf.

14 Ackroyd, 204.

15 Ibid., 235.

16 Ibid., 168.

17 Ibid., 287.

18 Ibid., 361.

19 Ibid., 255.

[20] Ibid., 369.

[21] Ibid., 330.

[22] William Roper, *The Life of Sir Thomas More* (New York: Barnes and Noble Books, 2005), 212.

[23] Ackroyd, 398, 405.

[24] Ibid., 373.

[25] Angel and Angel, 70.

[26] J.R.R. Tolkien, quoted in Patrick O'Hearn, *Courtship of the Saints* (TAN Books: Gastonia, NC, 2023), 251.

[27] *CCC*, 1615.

[28] Holböck, 319.

[29] Saint Thomas More, "A treatice upon the passion of Chryste," *Thomas More Studies*. Last modified, 2023. https://thomasmorestudies.org/wp-content/uploads/2020/08/Treatise_on_passion6-1.pdf.

Chapter 4: Loving Fruitfully

[1] *CCC*, 1832.

[2] "Luigi Beltrame Quattrocchi (1880-1951) and Maria Corsini Beltrame Quattrocchi (1884-1965)," The Holy See. www.vatican.va/news_services/liturgy/saints/ns_lit_doc_20011021_quattrocchi_it.html

[3] "Bl. Luigi Beltrame Quattrocchi and Bl. Maria Corsini," *L'Osservatore Romano*, October 10, 2001. See also www.ewtn.com/catholicism/library/bl-luigi-beltrame-quattrocchi-and-bl-maria-corsini-5630

[4] Dom Antoine Marie. "Luigi and Maria Beltrame Quattrocchi," *Abbaye Saint-Joseph de Clairval*, April 8, 2008, 1 www.clairval.com/documents/AN-2008-04-08.pdf.

[5] "Luigi Beltrame Quattrocchi (1880-1951) and Maria Corsini Beltrame Quattrocchi (1884-1965)."

[6] Joseph Lilgadas, *Santos y Santas 275: Luis y Maria Beltrame Quattrocchi* (Barcelona: Agpograf Impressors, 2020), 6.

[7] Letter from Luigi to Maria, July 29, 1905, as quoted in Lilgadas, 8.

[8] Dom Antoine Marie, 3.

[9] Ibid., 1.

[10] Lilgadas, 9.

[11] Dom Antoine Marie, 1.

[12] "Bl. Luigi Beltrame Quattrocchi and Bl. Maria Corsini."

[13] Mary Ann Sullivan, "Heroic in Marriage," *Marian Helper*, Spring 2002, 20-21.

[14] "Bl. Luigi Beltrame Quattrocchi and Bl. Maria Corsini."

[15] "The Spouses — A Story Together." *Luigi and Maria Beltrame Quattrocchi Association*, last modified 2023. www.luigiemaria.com/una-storia-insieme/

[16] Carol P. Kennedy, "Beautiful Together: Luigi Quattrocchi and Maria Corsini," *Lay Witness*, May/June 2002. 6-7.

[17] Pope John Paul II, "Beatification of the Servants of God Luigi Beltrame Quattrocchi and Maria Corsini, Married Couple," October 21, 2001, 2. http://w2.vatican.va/content/john-paul-ii/en/homilies/2001/documents/hf_jp-ii_hom_20011021_beltrame-quattrocchi.html.

[18] Sullivan.

[19] Pope John Paul II, "Beatification of the Servants of God," 2.

[20] Meg Hunter-Kilmer, "Blessed Luigi and Maria Quattrocchi: Ordinary married life, shot through with glory." *Aleteia*, November 25, 2017. https://aleteia.org/2017/11/25/blessed-luigi-and-maria-quattrocchi-ordinary-married-life-shot-through-with-glory.

[21] Dom Antoine Marie, 2.

[22] Ibid.

[23] Lilgadas, 18.

[24] Paola Dal Toso, "Luigi and Maria Beltrame Quattrocchi-Two Beatified Scouts," *Agescout*, Sept. 15, 2001. www.zio-zeb.it/beati_beltrame_quattrocchi.html.

[25] Hunter-Kilmer.

[26] "Bl. Luigi Beltrame Quattrocchi and Bl. Maria Corsini."

[27] Dom Antoine Marie, 4.

[28] "Bl. Luigi Beltrame Quattrocchi and Bl. Maria Corsini."

[29] *CCC*, 372.

[30] Pope Paul VI, *Humanae vitae*, 9.

[31] Angel and Angel, 115.

[32] Pope John Paul II, *Familiaris Consortio*, 33.

[33] Angel and Angel, 141.

[34] Pope Paul VI, *Humanae vitae*, 11

[35] Pope John Paul II, *Familiaris Consortio*, 36.

[36] Sullivan.

[37] "Spouses — Family Prayer." *Associate of Maria and Luigi*, last updated 2023. www.luigiemaria.com/preghiera-in-famiglia.

Chapter 5: For Better, For Worse

[1] Marg Mowczko, "All About Elizabeth (Luke 1)," Dec. 16, 2017. https://margmowczko.com/elizabeth-bible-woman-luke-1.

[2] Matthew G. Easton, "Easton's Bible Dictionary: Zacharias," 1897. https://en.wikisource.org/wiki/Easton%27s_Bible_Dictionary_(1897)/Zacharias.

[3] Holböck, 49.

[4] Mowczko.

[5] Susan J. Nelson, "Eight Life Lessons We Can Learn from Elizabeth in the Bible," *Woman of Noble Character*, October 28, 2019. www.womanofnoblecharacter.com/elizabeth-in-the-bible.

[6] Holböck, 48.

[7] "Holy Prophet Zachariah and Righteous Elizabeth, parents of Saint John the Baptist," *Orthodox Church in America*. www.oca.org/saints/lives/2020/09/05/102502-holy-prophet-zachariah-and-righteous-elizabeth-parents-of-saint.

[8] Gary Michuta, "Did John the Baptist's Father Die a Martyr?" *Detroit Catholic*, Sept. 2, 2016. www.detroitcatholic.com/voices/did-john-the-baptist-s-father-die-a-martyr

[9] "Holy Prophet Zachariah and Righteous Elizabeth, parents of Saint John the Baptist."

[10] See Lk 1:80; Lk 3:2-3; Mt 3:1.

[11] Bryan Cross, "A Catholic Reflection on the Meaning of Suffering," *Called to Communion*, Aug. 9, 2009. www.calledtocommunion.com/2009/08/a-catholic-reflection-on-the-meaning-of-suffering.

Chapter 6: For Richer, For Poorer

[1] Antonio Moore and Laura Moore, "For Richer...For Poorer – Money & Marriage," *Marriage Means Moore Inc*, March 12, 2020. https://marriagemeansmoore.com/for-richer-for-poorer-money-marriage.

[2] James Bogle and Joanna Bogle, *A Heart for Europe: The lives of Emperor Charles and Empress Zita of Austria-Hungary* (Harrisburg, PA: Morehouse Publishing, 1993), 1-8.

[3] *Butler's Lives of the Saints: Concise Edition* (San Francisco: Harper and Row, 1985), 124.

[4] Bogle and Bogle, 28.

[5] Ibid., 32.

[6] O'Hearn, 57.

[7] Bogle and Bogle, 35.

[8] Ibid., 40.

[9] "Who is Karl of Austria?" *Blessed Karl of Austria: Cause for Canonization USA/ Canada*, https://www.emperorcharles.org/biography

[10] Schloss Schönbrunn Kultur-und Betriebsges.m.b.H., "The World of the Habsburgs," 2020. www.habsburger.net/en./stories/pietas-austriaca.

[11] Bogle and Bogle, 9-10.

[12] See Pope Leo XIII, *Rerum Novarum*, May 15, 1891. www.vatican.va/content/leo-xiii/en/encyclicals/documents/hf_l-xiii_enc_15051891_rerum-novarum.html

[13] Brother Nathan Cochran, OSB, Blessed Karl of Austria: Novena, in The Emperor Karl League of Prayer USA and Canada, Edited by Msgr. Dr. Reinhard Knittel (no date), 27.

[14] Cristoph C Schönborn, "Who is Karl of Austria?" *Blessed Karl of Austria*. Last modified Oct. 3, 2004. www.emperorcharles.org/biography.

[15] Bogle and Bogle, 64.

[16] Bishop Robert Barron, "'1917,' War, and Faith," *Word on Fire Show*, Jan 27, 2020. www.youtube.com/watch?v=5tSD3-96yE8.

[17] Bogle and Bogle, 75-89.

[18] Ibid., 137.

[19] Hans Karl Zebner-Spitzenberg, *Death of an Emperor: Blessed Karl of Austria*, trans. Br. Nathan Cochran (Feldkirch: LINS Publishing House, 2004), 5.

[20] Bogle and Bogle, 141.

[21] Zebner-Spitzenberg, 16.

[22] Ibid., 19.

[23] Ibid., 13.

[24] Ibid., 14.

[25] Bogle and Bogle, 144.

[26] Ibid., 160.

[27] Seth B. Leonard, "The Great-Grandchildren of Emperor Karl and Empress Zita Who Have Taken Religious Orders," *Eurohistory*, Nov. 15, 2019. http://eurohistoryjournal.blogspot.com/2019/11/the-great-grandchildren-of-emperor-karl.html.

[28] Pope John Paul II. "Homily: Beatification of Five Servants of God." Oct. 3, 2004. www.vatican.va/content/john-paul-ii/en/homilies/2004/documents/hf_jp-ii_hom_20041003_beatifications.html

[29] Saint John Chrysostom, in *The Cult of the Saints: Select Homilies and Letters*, trans. Wendy Mayer and Bronwen Neil (Crestwood, NY: St. Vladimir Seminary Press, 2006), 247.

[30] See www.emperorcharles.org/prayers.

Chapter 7: In Sickness and In Health

[1] If their cause moves forward, their feast day will likely be their wedding anniversary, January 23.

[2] Annick Bescond, Olivier Rugamba, Dorcy Rugamba, Jean-Luc Moens, and Francois-Xavier Ngarambe, "J'Entrerai au Ciel en Dansant — Cyprien et Daphrose," Emmanuel Play, Dec. 28, 2016, YouTube, 26:40. www.youtube.com/watch?v=XYVhaLeZfqA.

[3] Ibid.

[4] Ibid.

[5] Ibid.

[6] Ibid.

[7] Jean-Luc Moens, personal interview, July 8, 2020.

[8] Bescond et. al.

[9] Ibid.

[10] Meg Hunter-Kilmer, "10 Married couples who have been canonized or are on their way," *Aleteia*, Feb. 15, 2020.
https://aleteia.org/2020/02/15/10-married-couples-who-have-been-canonized-or-are-on-their-way/

[11] Moens, personal interview.

[12] Bescond et. al.

[13] The Marian Fathers of the Immaculate Conception established their mission in Rwanda in 1984, and administer the Cana Formation Center in Kibeho, the site of the first Church-approved apparitions of Our Lady in Africa. The feast day of Our Lady of Kibeho is Nov. 28, the anniversary of the first apparition of Our Lady. Visit www.kibeho-cana.org.

[14] Moens, personal interview.

[15] "Who Are We?", *FidesCo Rwanda*. https://fidescorwanda.org/who-are-we/

[16] Bescond et. al.

[17] "What We Do," *Emmanuel Community*.
http://emmanuelcommunity.com/what-we-do.

[18] Bescond et. al.

[19] Ibid.

[20] "Rugamba Center. Kigali Rwanda," *Fidesco International*. www.fidesco-international.org/be/prj/centre-rugumba.

[21] Joshua J. McElwee, "Rwandan bishop carries special concerns to synod in Rome," *National Catholic Reporter*, Oct. 22, 2015. www.ncronline.org/news/vatican/rwandan-bishop-carries-special-concerns-synod-rome#

[22] Moens, personal interview.

[23] Ibid.

[24] Matthew S. Schwarz, Shankar Vedantam, and Tara Boyle, "Romeo & Juliet in Rwanda: How A Soap Opera Sought to Change a Nation," *NPR Hidden Brain Podcast*, July 13, 2020. www.npr.org/2020/07/13/890539487/romeo-juliet-in-rwanda-how-a-soap-opera-sought-to-change-a-nation.

[25] "Opening of the Causes for the Canonization of Cyprien and Daphrose Rugamba." *Emmanuel Community Blog*, Sept. 15, 2015. https://emmanuel.info/ouverture-des-causes-de-canonisation-de-cyprien-et-daphrose-rugamba.

[26] Claire Lesegretain, "Church Considers Holiness of Rwandan Couple," *La Croix*, Sept. 16, 2015. www.la-croix.com/Religion/Actualite/L-Eglise-se-penche-sur-la-saintete-d-un-couple-rwandais-2015-09-16-1357038.

[27] Bescond et. al.

[28] Pope John Paul II. "Address to a Group of Officials in the Nyamirambo Stadium," September 8, 1990. www.vatican.va/content/john-paul-ii/it/speeches/1990/september/documents/hf_jp-ii_spe_19900908_stadio-nyamirambo.html

[29] Moens., personal interview.

[30] *CCC*, 1443.

[31] Archbishop of Kigali. Reprinted with written permission.

Chapter 8: 'Til Death Do Us Part

[1] Giovanni Falbo, *St. Monica: The Power of a Mother's Love* (Boston: Pauline Books and Media, 2007), 6-9.

[2] Augustine of Hippo, *Confessions*, 148.

[3] Falbo, 10-12.

[4] Ibid., 18-21.

[5] Ibid., 18.

[6] Holböck, 173-4.

[7] Falbo, 24.

[8] Ibid., 21.

[9] Ibid., 30.

[10] Ibid., 37.

[11] Augustine of Hippo, "A Treatise on the Merits and Forgiveness of Sins, and on the Baptism of Infants," in *Saint Augustin: Anti-Pelagian Writings*, ed. Philip Schaff, trans. Peter Holmes, vol. 5, A Select Library of the Nicene and Post-Nicene Fathers of the Christian Church, First Series (New York: Christian Literature Company, 1887), 72.

[12] Saint Augustine, *Confessions*, 72.

[13] Ibid., 33-46.

[14] Ibid., 43.

[15] Ibid., 44.

[16] Falbo, 46.

[17] Saint Augustine, *Confessions*, 12.

[18] Falbo, 52.

[19] Saint Augustine, *Confessions*, 79.

[20] Falbo, 60.

[21] Ibid., 65.

[22] Ibid., 72-3.

[23] *Butler's Lives of the Saints*, 267.

[24] Saint Augustine, *Confessions*, 136.

[25] Falbo, 82.

[26] Ibid., 82-83.

[27] Saint Augustine, *Confessions*, 153.

[28] Falbo, 107.

[29] Saint Augustine, *Confessions*, 152.

[30] Ibid., 154.

[31] Falbo, 135.

[32] Ibid., 111.

[33] *CCC*, 2299.

[34] Ibid., 1010.

[35] Ibid., 1007.

[36] Saint Augustine, *Confessions*, 158.

[37] Saint Augustine, "Prayer of Trust in God's Heavenly Promise," as quoted in *Friends of St. Augustine — Prayer Resource Guide*, March 10, 2015. www.osa.org.au/media/30007/2015B.pdf.

Chapter 9: The Most Exemplary Marriage of All Time

[1] Pope John Paul II, *Familiaris Consortio*, 61.

[2] Michael Ruszala, "Stories about the Birth and Childhood of the Blessed Virgin Mary," *Ascension Press*, Sept. 8, 2020. https://media.ascensionpress.com/2020/09/08/stories-about-the-birth-and-childhood-of-the-blessed-virgin-mary.

[3] See www.catholic.com/audio/ddp/the-year-jesus-was-born.

[4] Father Donald Calloway, MIC, *Consecration to St. Joseph: The Wonders of Our Spiritual Father* (Stockbridge, MA: Marian Press, 2020), 113.

[5] Venerable Mary of Agreda, quoted in O'Hearn, 38.

[6] Jimmy Akin, "The Genealogies of Christ," *Catholic Answers*, Dec. 1, 1997. www.catholic.com/magazine/print-edition/the-genealogies-of-christ.

[7] Calloway, 84.

[8] Cardinal Raymond Leo Burke, "The Marriage of Saint Joseph and the Blessed Virgin Mary, and the Mystery of the Redemptive Incarnation," *Missio Immaculatae*, June 15, 2021. https://missiomagazine.com/the-marriage-of-saint-joseph-and-the-blessed-virgin-mary-and-the-mystery-of-the-redemptive-incarnation.

[9] Calloway, 143-6.

[10] Pope Francis, *Patris Corde*, Dec. 8, 2020, 7. www.vatican.va/content/francesco/en/apost_letters/documents/papa-francesco-lettera-ap_20201208_patris-corde.html

[11] *CCC*, 506.

[12] United States Conference of Catholic Bishops, *Marriage: Love and Life in the Divine Plan* (Washington, DC: USCCB Publishing, 2009), 53-4. www.usccb.org/resources/pastoral-letter-marriage-love-and-life-in-the-divine-plan.pdf

[13] Hahn, *Hail, Holy Queen*, 45.

[14] Ibid., 59.

[15] *CCC*, 963.

[16] Pope Francis, *Patris Corde*, 7

[17] Calloway, 198.

[18] Ibid., 163-4.

[19] Ibid., 165-6.

[20] Father Ed Broom, OSV, "The 5 Advent Virtues of St. Joseph," *The Catholic Gentleman*, Dec. 20, 2014. https://catholicgentleman.net/2014/12/5-advent-virtues-st-joseph.

[21] Ibid.

22 Hahn, *Signs of Life*, 56.

23 *CCC*, 964.

24 As quoted in Calloway, 103.

25 Hahn, *Hail, Holy Queen*, 166.

26 Calloway, 89.

27 Ibid., 191-207.

28 Ibid., 2.

29 Ibid., 222.

30 Pope Francis, *Amoris Laetitia*, 325.

Conclusion

1 Pope John Paul II, "Homily: Puebla de Los Angeles (Mexico), Palafox Major Seminary," Jan. 28, 1979. www.vatican.va/content/john-paul-ii/en/homilies/1979/documents/hf_jp-ii_hom_19790128_messico-puebla-seminario.html

2 David Anders, *The Catholic Church Saved My Marriage: Discovering Hidden Grace in the Sacrament of Matrimony* (Irondale, AL: EWTN Publishing, Inc., 2018), 159.

3 *CCC*, 1624.

4 Father Joseph Sicardo, OSA, *St. Rita of Cascia: Saint of the Impossible* (Rockford, IL: TAN, 1990), 31-3.

5 Ibid., 55.

6 "Life of Saint Rita of Cascia," January 2023. https://santaritadacascia.org/la-santa/vita.

7 Sicardo, 63, 67.

8 Ibid., 148.

9 Hahn, *Signs of Life*, 69.

10 *Marriage: Love and Life in the Divine Plan*, 6.

11 *CCC*, 1613.

12 Scott Hahn, *First Comes Love: Finding Your Family in the Church and the Trinity* (New York: Doubleday, 2002), 67.

13 Pope Francis, *Amoris Laetitia*, 11.

14 Carol P. Kennedy, "Beautiful Together: Luigi Quattrocchi and Maria Corsini," *Lay Witness*, May/June 2002, 6-7.

15 Rick Santorum, "The Necessity of Marriage," *The Heritage Foundation*, Oct. 20, 2003. www.heritage.org/marriage-and-family/report/the-necessity-marriage

16 Pope Francis, *Amoris Laetitia*, 52.

17 www.usccb.org/prayers/prayer-defense-marriage.

Enriching Reading for the Entire Family

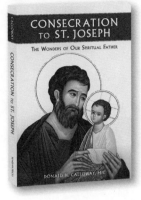

Consecration to St. Joseph:
The Wonders of Our Spiritual Father

In the midst of crisis, confusion, and a world at war with the Church, it's time to come home again to our spiritual father, St. Joseph. In this richly researched and lovingly presented program of consecration to St. Joseph, Fr. Donald Calloway, MIC, brings to life the wonders, the power, and the ceaseless love of St. Joseph, Patron of the Universal Church and the Terror of Demons. Paperback. 320 pages. Y124-FCSJ [e] Spanish: Y124-SCSJ

Consecration to St. Joseph for Children and Families

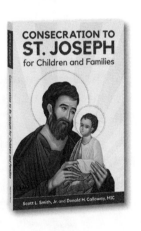

Protect your family! Entrust your family to St. Joseph. Why? Because God, Himself, did. God entrusted the Holy Family to St. Joseph to keep them safe, and so should you. Drawing on the wealth of the Church's living tradition, Fr. Calloway and co-author Scott L. Smith, Jr., call on all of us to turn to St. Joseph, entrust ourselves, our children and families, our Church, and our world to our spiritual father's loving care. Watch for wonders when the Universal Patron of the Church opens the floodgates of Heaven to pour out graces into your family's lives. Paperback. 160 pages. Y124-CJHB

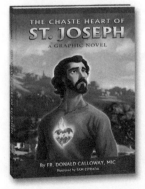

The Chaste Heart of Joseph
A Graphic Novel

How much do you really know about St. Joseph? He was once a little boy and played like all children. He had royal blood, and could have been a king. He was a young man when he married Mary. He was the brave and steadfast protector of the Holy Family. He's the model of manhood ... and he had a pure, chaste heart. Join Fr. Donald Calloway, MIC, as he tells the dynamic and inspiring story of St. Joseph, our spiritual father and the "Terror of Demons," in this unique graphic novel for all ages, illustrated by Sam Estrada. Hardcover. 84 pages. Y124-JOEG

Call 1-800-462-7426 or ShopMercy.org

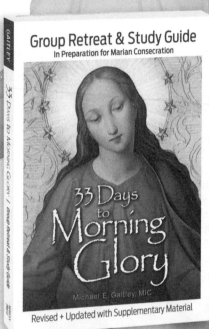

The "Gems" Series of Daily Devotionals

Bible Gems
Scripture Verses on God's Mercy and Overcoming Fear

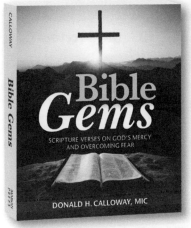

By Fr. Donald H. Calloway, MIC

Perfect love casts out fear, and God is love (see 1 Jn 4:16-19). So let us allow His Word to find a home in our hearts each day with these 366 Scriptural exhortations to fear not, as we journey through the books of the Bible using verses drawn from the *Divine Mercy Catholic Bible* (Revised Standard Version — Catholic Edition 2). "Do not be afraid," perhaps the most well-known phrase of the pontificate of Pope St. John Paul II, comes across very strongly in these daily reflections. It's a message that is timeless and brings comfort to the heart. Paperback. 360 pages. Y124-GEMB

Sacred Heart Gems: Daily Wisdom on the Heart of Jesus
Y124-SHGM

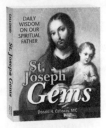

St. Joseph Gems: Daily Wisdom on Our Spiritual Father
Y124-SJEM

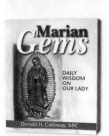

Eucharistic Gems: Daily Wisdom on the Blessed Sacrament
Y124-EUGM

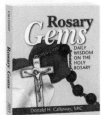

Marian Gems: Daily Wisdom on Our Lady
Y124-MGEM

Rosary Gems: Daily Wisdom on the Holy Rosary
Y124-RGEM

Call 1-800-462-7426 or ShopMercy.org

Join the
Association of Marian Helpers,
headquartered at the
National Shrine of The Divine Mercy,
and share in special blessings!

**An invitation from
Fr. Joseph, MIC, the director**

**Marian Helpers is an Association of
Christian faithful of the Congregation
of Marian Fathers of the
Immaculate Conception.**
By becoming a member, you
share in the spiritual benefits
of the daily Masses, prayers,
and good works of the Marian
priests and brothers.

This is a special offer of grace
given to you by the Church
through the Marians. Please consider this opportunity to
share in these blessings, along with others whom you would
wish to join into this spiritual communion.

The Marian Fathers of the Immaculate Conception of the
Blessed Virgin Mary is a religious congregation of nearly
500 priests and brothers around the world.

Call 1-800-462-7426 or visit Marian.org

Give a Consoling Gift: *Prayer*

Enroll your loved ones in the Association of Marian Helpers, and they will participate in the graces from the daily Masses, prayers, good works, and merits of the Marian priests and brothers around the world.

1-800-462-7426
Marian.org/enrollments

Enrollments can be offered for the living or deceased. We offer a variety of enrollment cards: wedding, anniversary, First Holy Communion, birthday, get well, and more.

Request a Mass
to be offered by the Marian Fathers for your loved one

Individual Masses
(for the living or deceased)

Gregorian Masses
(30 days of consecutive Masses for the deceased)

1-800-462-7426
Marian.org/mass